PROGRAMMING IN C(KTU Syllabus)

```
Happiness
is {
    a day
    spent
    coding();
}
```

AF661163

Dr. Arun Anoop M

Associate Professor,
Dept. of Computer Science & Engineering,
Alva's Institute of Engineering & Technology,
Moodubidire, Karnataka, India

Dr. Manjunath Kotari

Professor& Head,
Dept. of Computer Science & Engineering,
Alva's Institute of Engineering & Technology,
Moodubidire, Karnataka, India

SHANLAX PUBLICATIONS

Title:	PROGRAMMING IN C (KTU Syllabus)
Author Names:	Dr. Arun Anoop M Dr. Manjunath Kotari
Published by:	Shanlax Publications, Vasantha Nagar, Madurai - 625003, Tamil Nadu, India
Publisher's Address:	61, 66 T.P.K. Main Road, Vasantha Nagar, Madurai - 625003, Tamil Nadu, India
Printer's Details:	Shanlax Press, 66 T.P.K. Main Road, Vasantha Nagar, Madurai - 625003, Tamil Nadu, India
Edition Details (I,II,III):	I
ISBN:	978-93-94899-66-7
Month & Year:	July, 2022
Copyright @	Dr. Arun Anoop M Dr. Manjunath Kotari
Pages:	128
Price:	₹240

PREFACE

This book covers KTU university basedlab experiments in Computer Science & Engineering. This book is presented in simple and easily understandable manner. This book, I hope will be very useful for all engineering students for practical examinations of CSE department. I have made a humble attempt in this book to support students to pass the practical exams.

The book is structured to cover the key aspects of major topics in the subject. It is specially designed to meet the expectations of KeralaTechnological University(APJ Abdul Kalam Technological University).

All care has been taken to make students comfortable in understanding the important concepts.

ACKNOWLEDGEMENT

First of all I would like to thank my Parents for showering their blessings upon me to pursue this book work. The words cannot describe their role in my life, I cannot think of living without their love and care without which I could not have carried out this book work.

I sincerely thank Hon'ble DR. M. MOHAN ALVA, Chairman, Alva's Education Foundation and Shri. Vivek Alva for their constant source of inspiration , guidance and blessings to all my efforts.

I express my sincere thanks to Hon'ble Principal, Dr. Peter Fernandes, ALVA'S INSTITUTE OF ENGINEERING &TECHNOLOGY, Moodubidire, Karnataka for their visionary support and guidance in bringing outcomes for all my efforts.

I wish to express my hearty thanks and deep sense of gratitude to the all HODs , staff members and my dear students for their encouragement and support.

My sincere gratitude goes to my beloved Research guide Dr. S. Poonkuntran, Professor & Dean, School of Computer Science & Engineering, VIT University, Sehore, Bhopal and my Research coordinator Dr. P. Karthikeyan, Associate Professor, Department of ECE and HoD of CSE & ECE department, Velammal College of Engineering and Technology (VCET), Madurai for their blessings and support.

My sincere gratitude goes to my beloved Dr. V. Vasudevan, Registrar, Kalasalingam University for their unbounded support in shaping all my efforts.

I sincerely thank my sister Mrs. AGIJA and my brother in law Mr. Anil, for their blessings to make this book a reality.

Dr. Arun Anoop M.

CONTENTS

PROGRAMMING IN C

Introductions

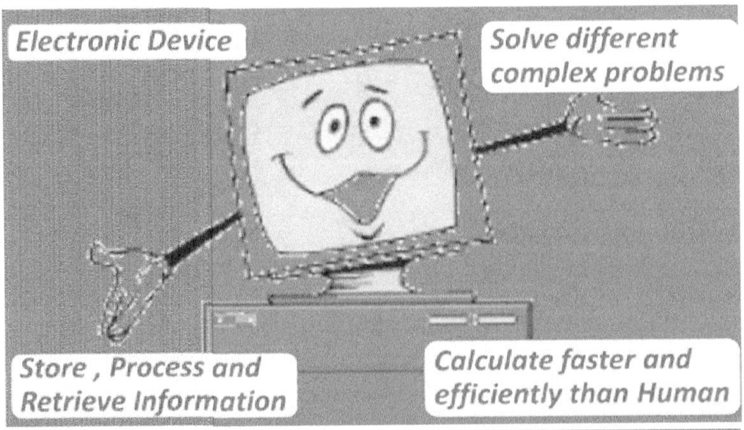

10
FIRST COMPUTER
ABACUS

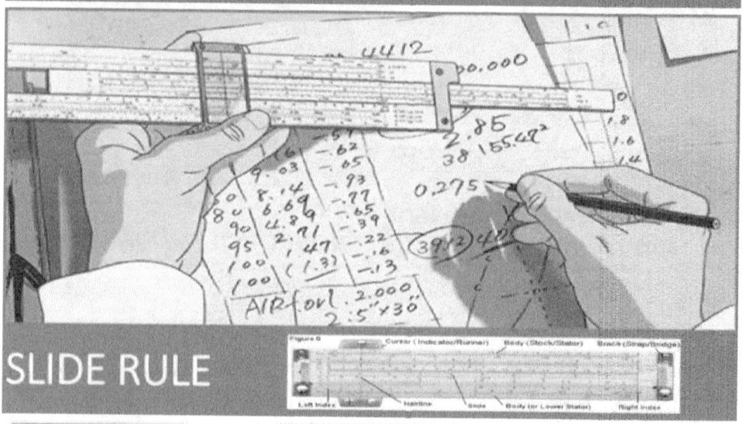
SLIDE RULE

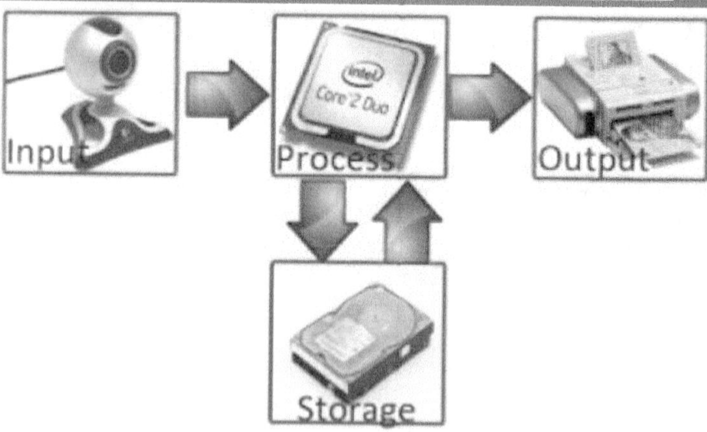
Input
Process
Output
Storage

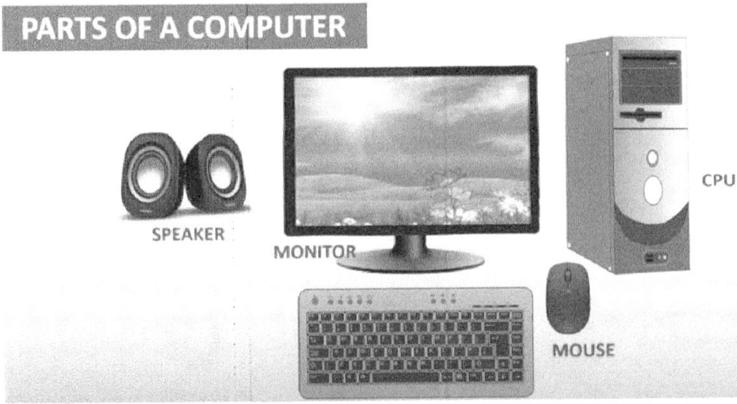
PARTS OF A COMPUTER
SPEAKER
MONITOR
CPU
MOUSE

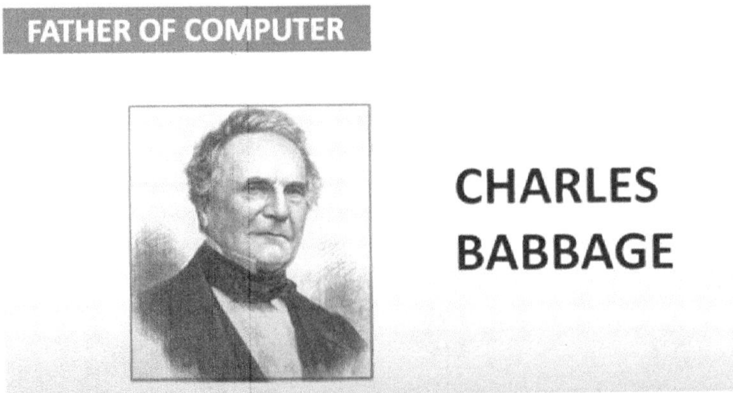
FATHER OF COMPUTER
CHARLES
BABBAGE

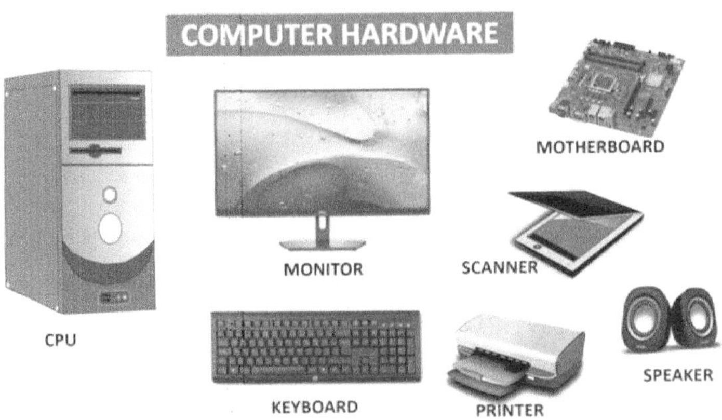
COMPUTER HARDWARE
MOTHERBOARD
MONITOR
SCANNER
CPU
SPEAKER
KEYBOARD
PRINTER

HOW A COMPUTER WORKS?

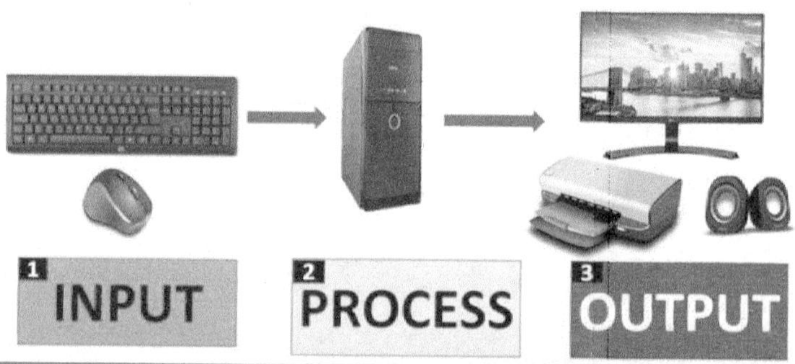

INPUT
PROCESS
OUTPUT
FRUITS
THE JUICER PROCESS THE FRUITS
JUICE

EXAMPLE

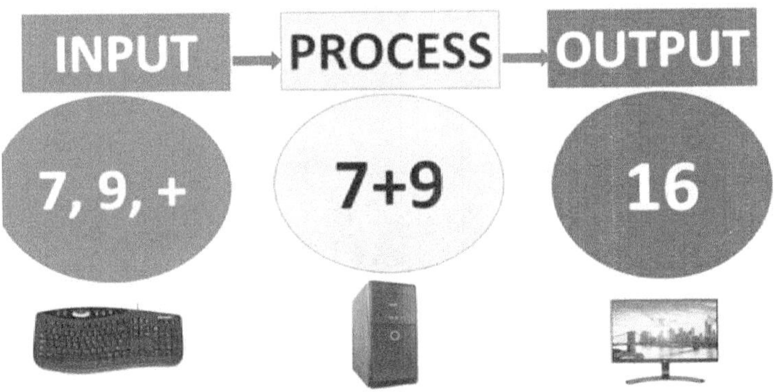
INPUT
PROCESS
OUTPUT
7, 9, +
7+9
16

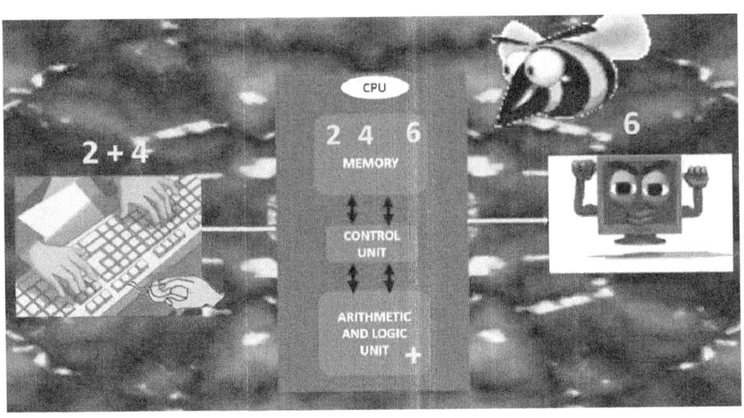
2 + 4
CPU
2 4 6
MEMORY
CONTROL UNIT
ARITHMETIC AND LOGIC UNIT
6

INPUT DEVICES

KEYBOARD

MOUSE

JOYSTICK

MICROPHONE

LIGHT PEN

SCANNER

OUTPUT DEVICES

MONITOR

PRINTER

PROJECTOR

HEADPHONES

SPEAKER

COMPUTER LANGUAGE

MACHINE LANGUAGE OR LOW-LEVEL LANGUAGE

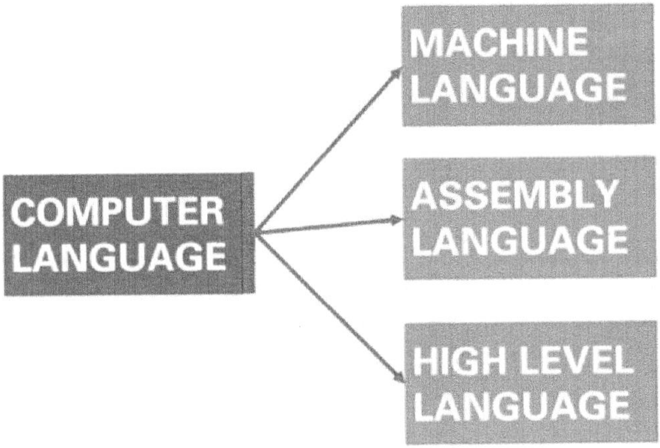
COMPUTER LANGUAGE
MACHINE LANGUAGE
ASSEMBLY LANGUAGE
HIGH LEVEL LANGUAGE

USES OF COMPUTER
STUDY
MUSIC
WATCH MOVIE
PLAY GAMES
DRAW
CHAT
SEND E-MAILS
SURF THE INTERNET

COMPUTER IN OUR DAILY LIFE

SCHOOLS

HOSPITALS

OFFICES

HOME

BANKS

AIRPORTS

ADVANTAGES OF COMPUTER

ACCURATE

NOT TIRED

MULTITASKING

NEVER FORGETS

FAST

DISADVANTAGES OF COMPUTER

NO FEELINGS

CAN'T DECIDE

WORKS ON USER'S ORDER

Why we need
Computer
Language ?

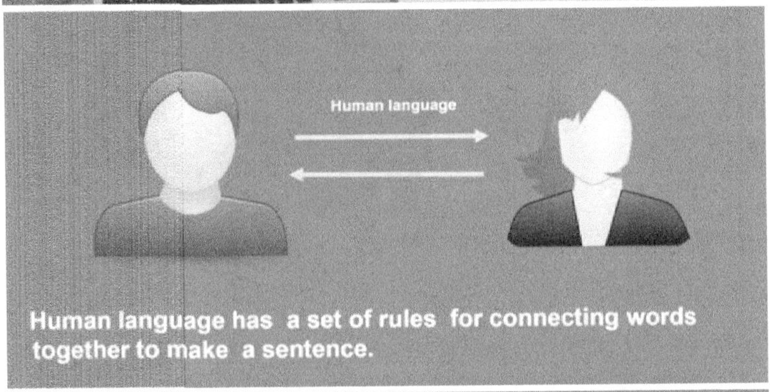
Human language
Human language has a set of rules for connecting words together to make a sentence.

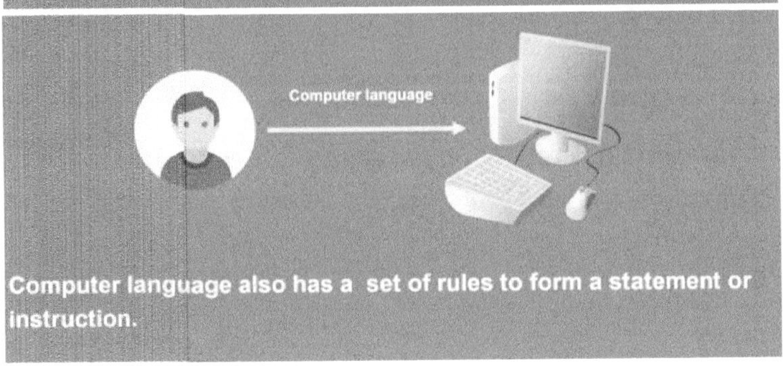
Computer language
Computer language also has a set of rules to form a statement or instruction.

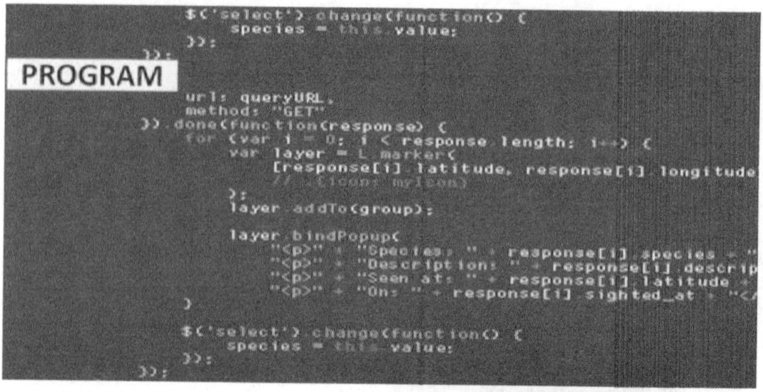

Humans can't directly communicate with computers

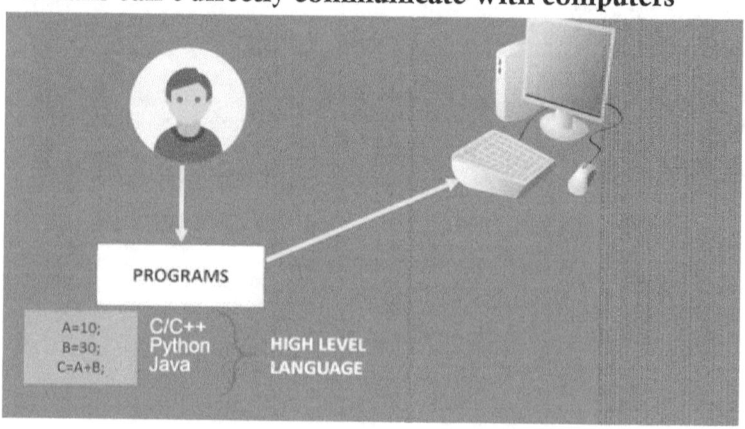

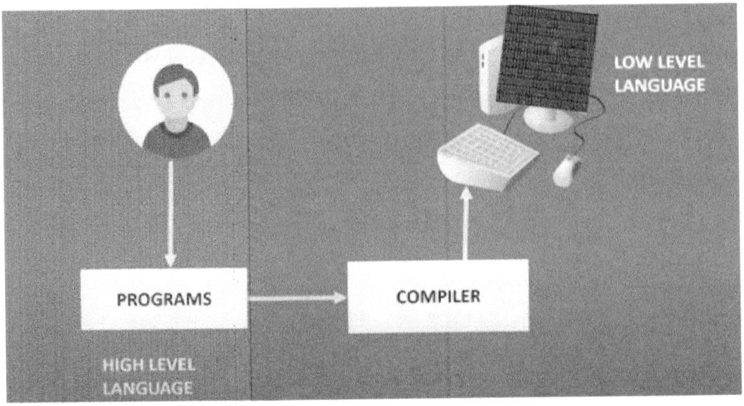
LOW LEVEL
LANGUAGE
PROGRAMS
COMPILER
HIGH LEVEL
LANGUAGE

HUMAN
UNDERSTABLE
LANGUAGE
TRANSLATOR
PROGRAM
MACHINE
UNDERSTANBLE
LANGUAGE
SOURCE
CODE
OBJECT
CODE

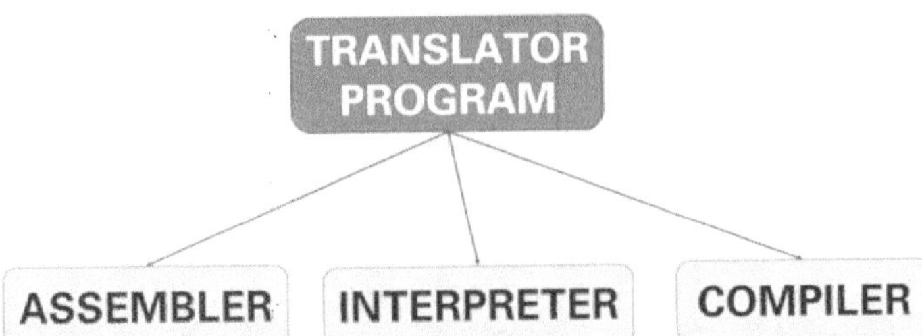
TRANSLATOR
PROGRAM
ASSEMBLER
INTERPRETER
COMPILER

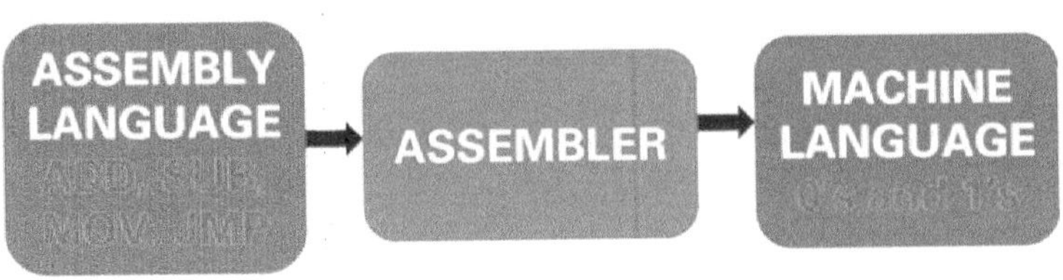
ASSEMBLY
LANGUAGE
ASSEMBLER
MACHINE
LANGUAGE

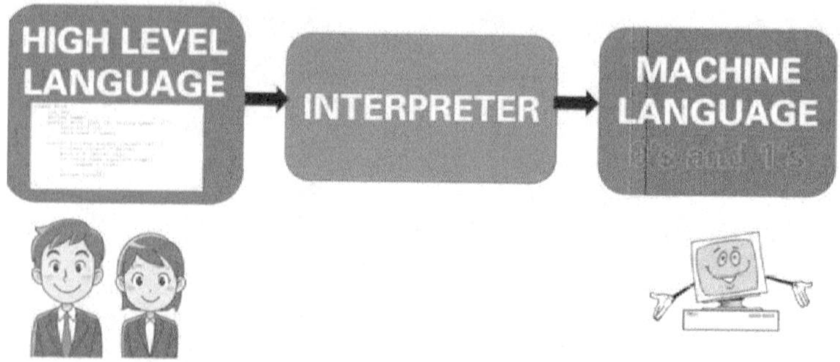

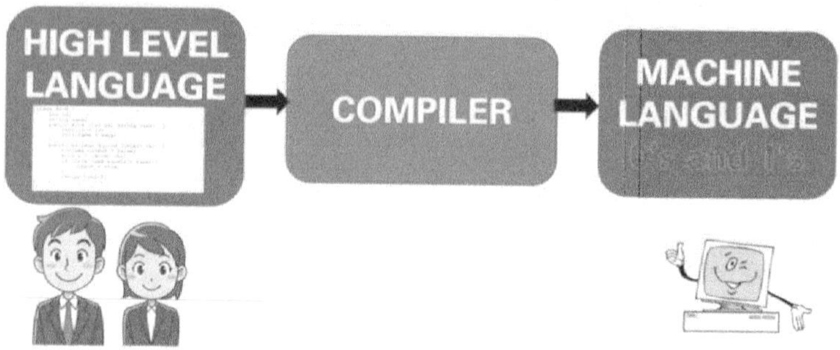

Computer Programming:

- Set of instructions
- It helps the programmer to perform specific tasks
- Return desired output for the valid inputs
- Input(s) → Program → Output(tasks)
- Process of designing and developing executable computer programs to perform specific tasks.
- Programming: is the process of writing programs or software's.

Given below is a Mathematical Expression.

Z = X + Y, where X, Y, and Z are the variables in a programming language.
If X = 550 and Y = 450, the value of X and Y are the input values that are called literals.
We ask the computer to calculate the value of X+Y, which results in Z, i.e. the expected output.

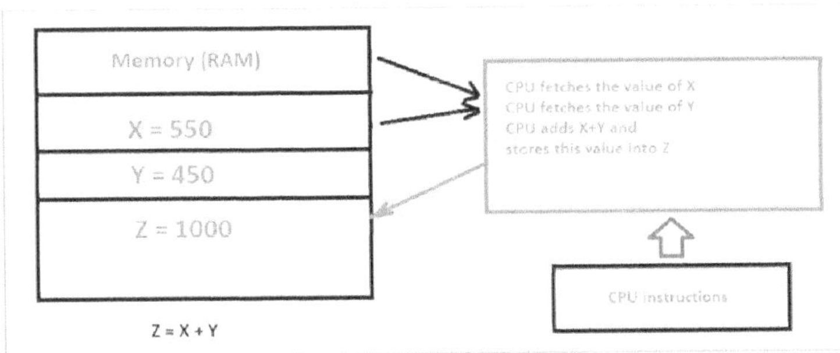

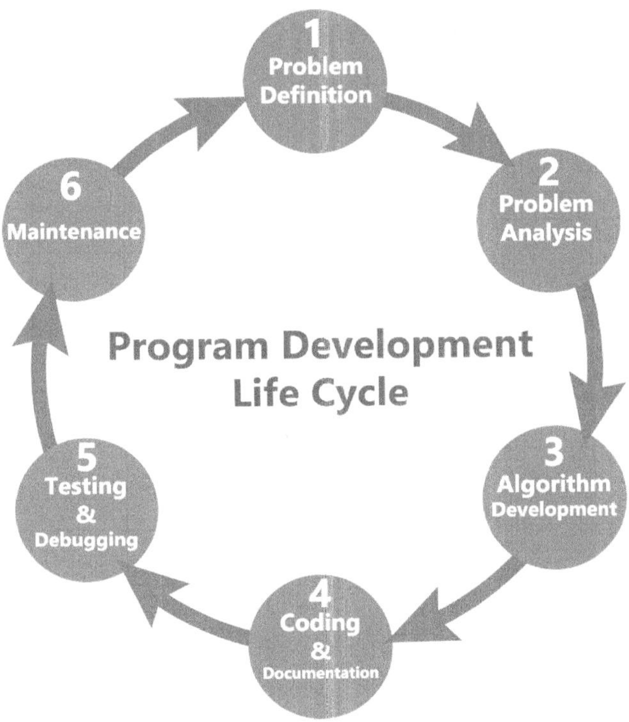

- **Debugging** - *Done by Development Team* - The task of finding and removing errors/bugs from the program.
- **Testing** - *Done by Testing Team* - The task of locating and identifying of bugs/errors included

- Syntax - error relating to the programming language used
- Logical - error in programming logic
- Run-time/execution - error that appears after you compile and run your code

Dr.Arun Anoop M

1. Problem Definition
2. Problem Analysis
3. Algorithm Development
4. Coding & Documentation
5. Testing & Debugging
6. Maintenance

1. Problem Definition: (1) Understand the problem statement (2)Our requirements(3) Output of problem solution
2. Problem Analysis: (1) requirements to solve the problem. (2) Gather the required solutions to solve the problem.
3. Algorithm development: (1)Step by step sequence to solve the problem. (2) Write solution in step by step statement.
4. Coding & documentation: (1) Write programs. (2) Write programs to solve the problem.
5. Testing & debugging: (1) Check whether code is written for solving specified problem or not (2) Test whether it is solving the problem for valid inputs or not (3) Test whether it is solving the desired outputs or not.
6. Maintenance: (1) Program is actively used by users (2) Program is used by end users.(3) If user encounters any problem, need to repeat all the phases from the beginning, so that encountered problem is solved.

Introduction to Algorithms:

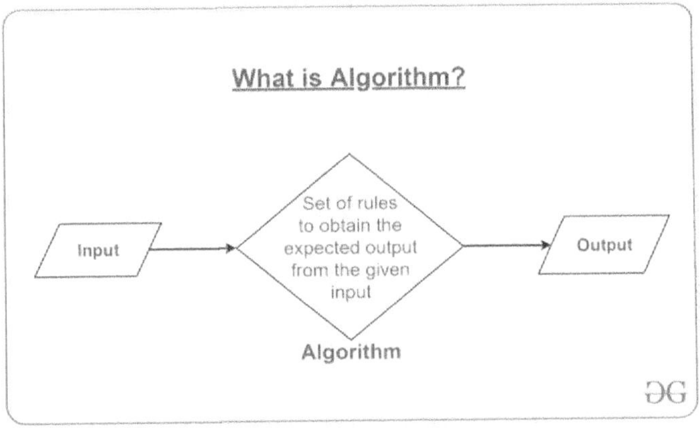

- The word Algorithm means "a process or set of rules based on logic steps.Therefore Algorithm refers to a set of rules/instructions that step-by-step define how a work is to be executed to get the expected results.
- It can be understood by taking an example of baking a new biscuit. To bake a new biscuit, one reads the instructions and steps and execute them one by one, in the given sequence. The result thus obtained is the new dish baked perfectly. Similarly, algorithms help to do a task in programming to get the expected output.
- The Algorithm designed are language-independent, i.e. they are just plain instructions that can be implemented in any language, and yet the output will be the same, as expected.
- An algorithm is a set of steps designed to solve a problem or accomplish a task.
- Algorithms are usually written in pseudocode, or a combination of high level or speaking language and one or more programming languages, in advance of writing a program.
- Our translators, will translate these high level programs to machine level language either 0 or 1.

- Machine can understand only their language codes. Human can understand codes only if it's in high level language.
- We can train babies, so gradually babies can identify each and every terms based on some conditions and representations.
- Likewise, computers can understand every thing based on programmer's representations, especially based on the logic of programs.
- We are giving inputs by using input device(keyboard), reading output data from our monitor, type of output device.

Algorithm 1: Add two numbers entered by the user

```
Step 1: Start
Step 2: Declare variables num1, num2 and sum.
Step 3: Read values num1 and num2.
Step 4: Add num1 and num2 and assign the result to sum.
        sum←num1+num2
Step 5: Display sum
Step 6: Stop
```

Algorithm 2: Find the largest number among three numbers

```
Step 1: Start
Step 2: Declare variables a,b and c.
Step 3: Read variables a,b and c.
Step 4: If a > b
           If a > c
              Display a is the largest number.
           Else
              Display c is the largest number.
        Else
           If b > c
              Display b is the largest number.
           Else
              Display c is the greatest number.
Step 5: Stop
```

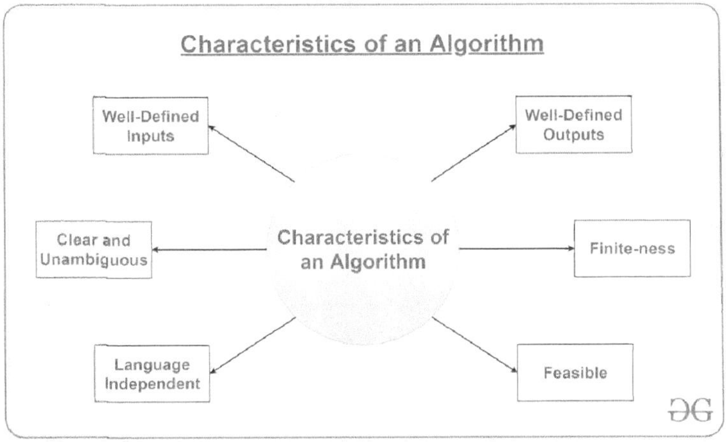

- Clear and Unambiguous: Algorithm should be clear and unambiguous. Each of its steps should be clear in all aspects and must lead to only one meaning.
- Well-Defined Inputs: If an algorithm says to take inputs, it should be well-defined inputs.
- Well-Defined Outputs: The algorithm must clearly define what output will be yielded and it should be well-defined as well.
- Finite-ness: The algorithm must be finite, i.e. it should not end up in an infinite loops or similar.
- Feasible: The algorithm must be simple, generic and practical, such that it can be executed upon will the available resources. It must not contain some future technology, or anything.
- Language Independent: The Algorithm designed must be language-independent, i.e. it must be just plain instructions that can be implemented in any language, and yet the output will be same, as expected.

Symbol	Name	Function
	Start/end	An oval represents a start or end point
	Arrows	A line is a connector that shows relationships between the representative shapes
	Input/Output	A parallelogram represents input or output
	Process	A rectangle represents a process
	Decision	A diamond indicates a decision

Example 1: Print 1 to 20:

Algorithm:

- Step 1: Initialize X as 0,
- Step 2: Increment X by 1,
- Step 3: Print X,
- Step 4: If X is less than 20 then go back to step 2.

Flowchart:

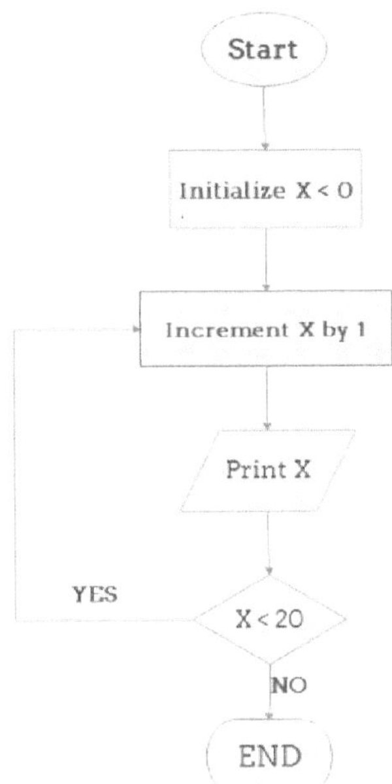

Determine Whether A Student Passed the Exam or Not:

Algorithm:

- Step 1: Input grades of 4 courses M1, M2, M3 and M4,
- Step 2: Calculate the average grade with formula "Grade=(M1+M2+M3+M4)/4"
- Step 3: If the average grade is less than 60, print "FAIL", else print "PASS".

Flowchart:

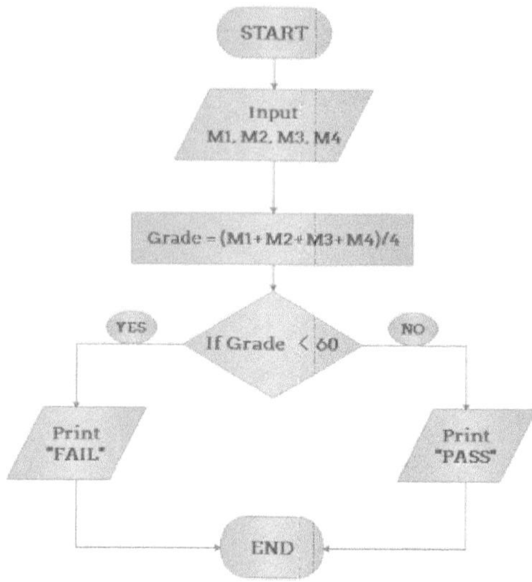

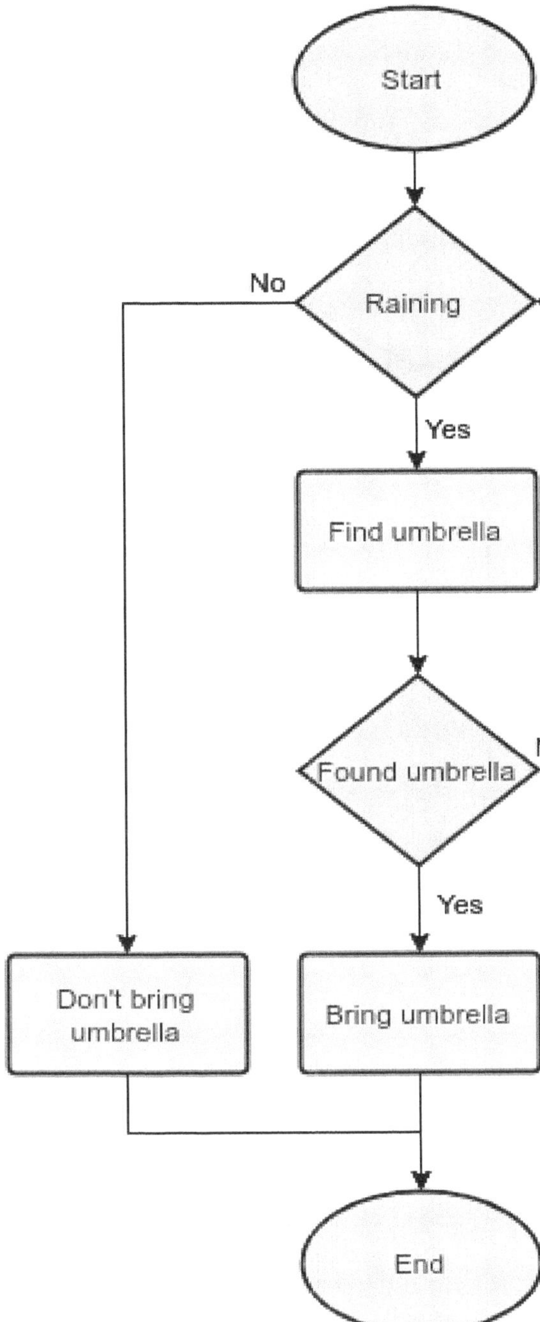
Start
Raining
No
Yes
Find umbrella
Found umbrella
No
Yes
Don't bring umbrella
Bring umbrella
End

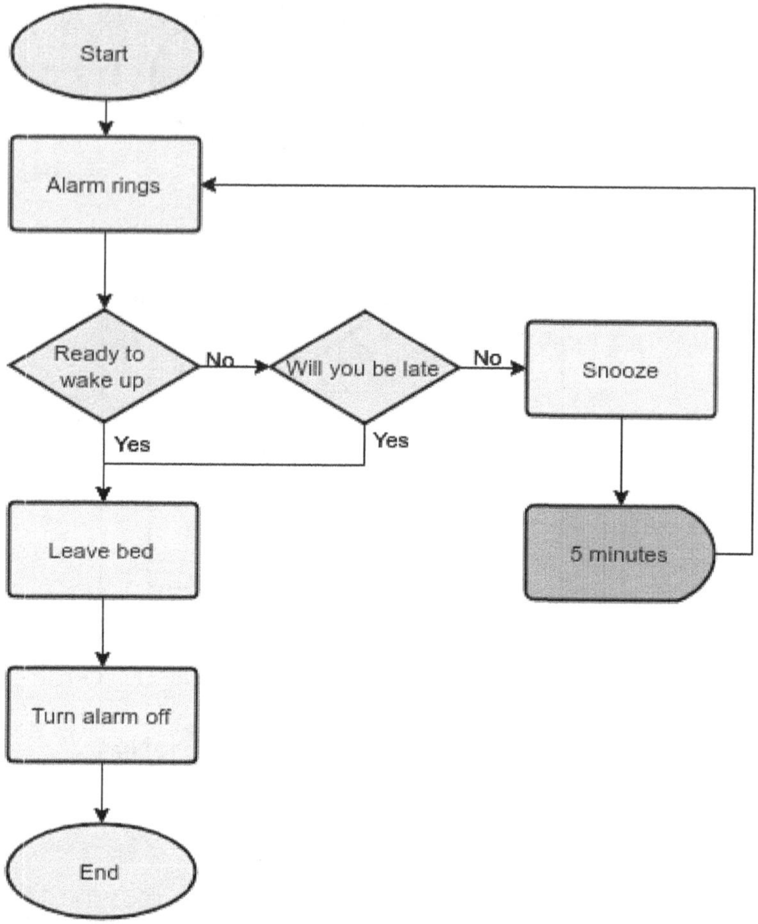
Start
Alarm rings
Ready to wake up
No
Will you be late
No
Snooze
Yes
Yes
Leave bed
5 minutes
Turn alarm off
End

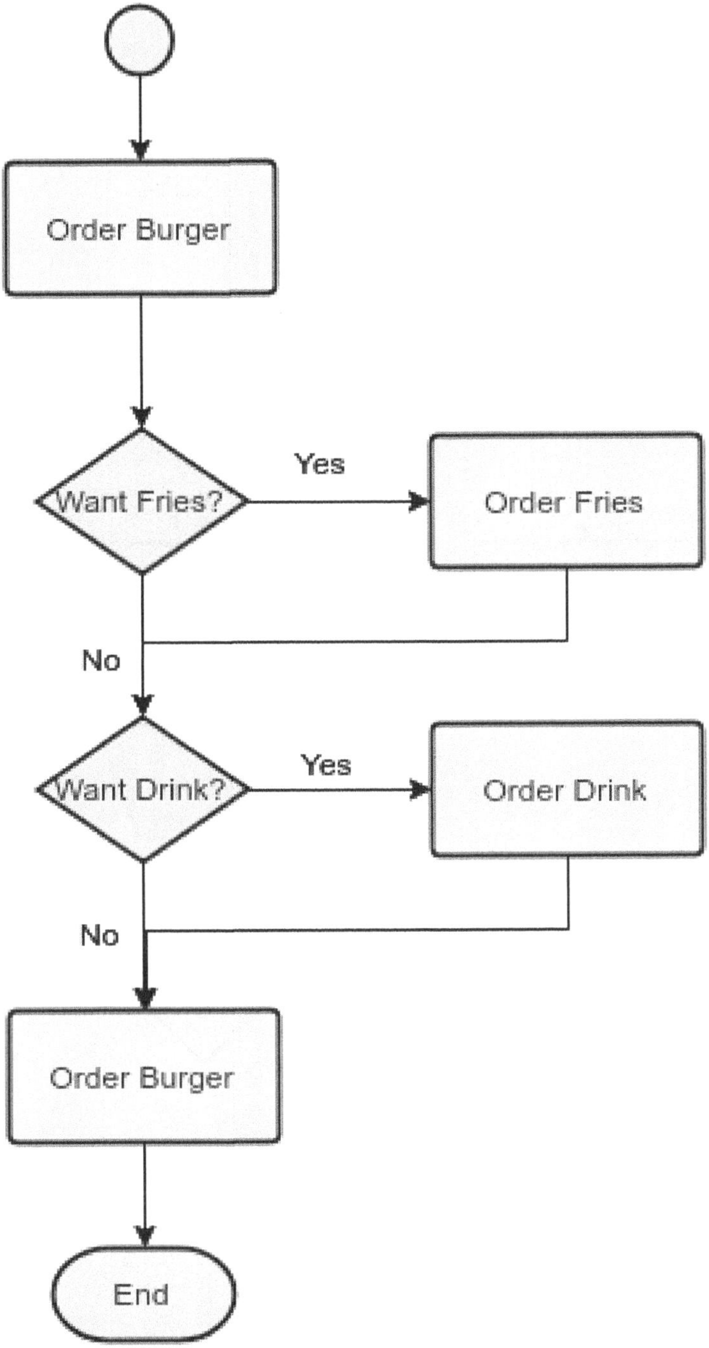
Order Burger
Want Fries?
Yes
Order Fries
No
Want Drink?
Yes
Order Drink
No
Order Burger
End

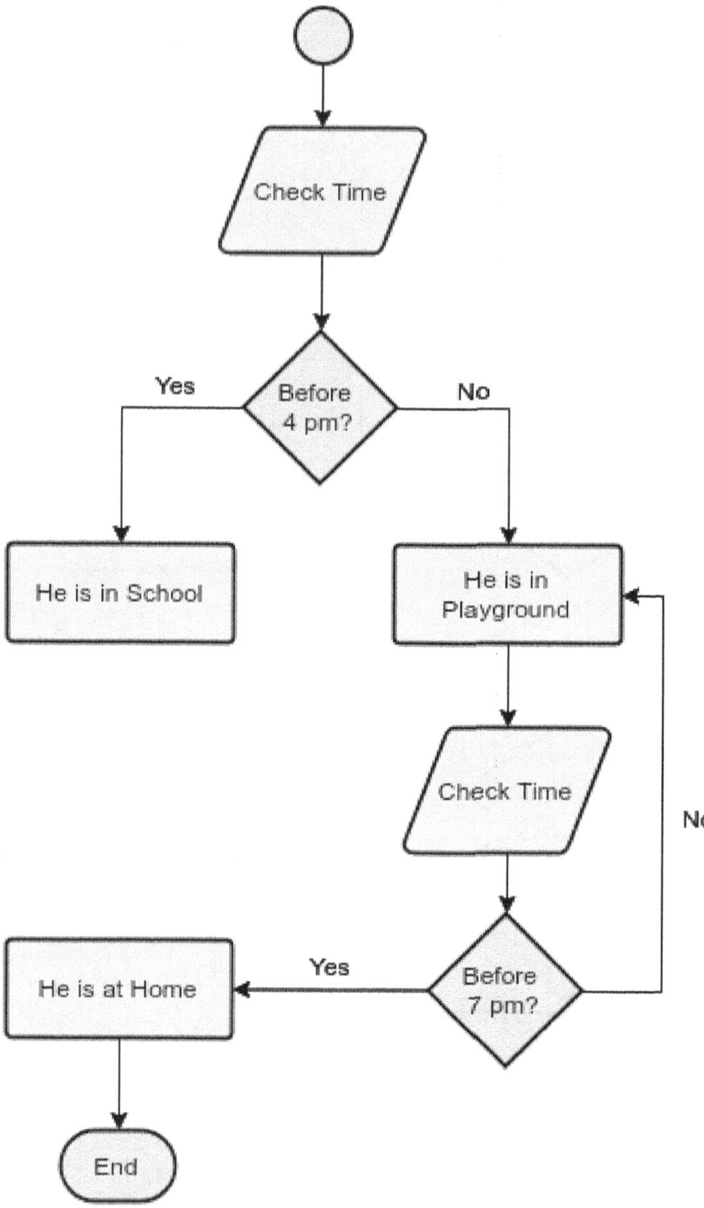
Check Time
Yes
Before 4 pm?
No
He is in School
He is in Playground
Check Time
No
Yes
He is at Home
Before 7 pm?
End

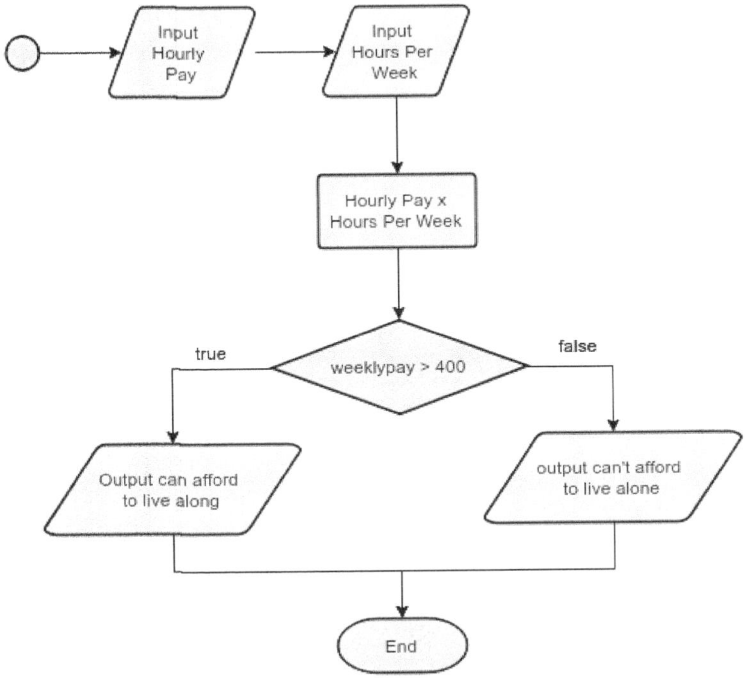
Input
Hourly
Pay
Input
Hours Per
Week
Hourly Pay x
Hours Per Week
weeklypay > 400
true
false
Output can afford
to live along
output can't afford
to live alone
End

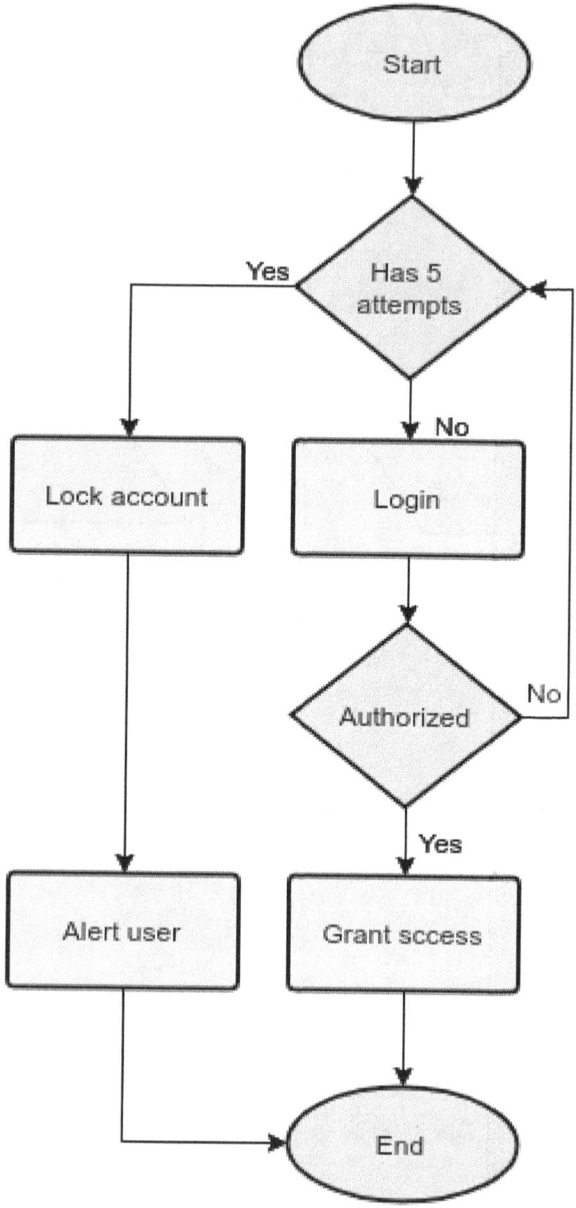
Start
Has 5 attempts
Yes
No
Lock account
Login
Authorized
No
Yes
Alert user
Grant sccess
End

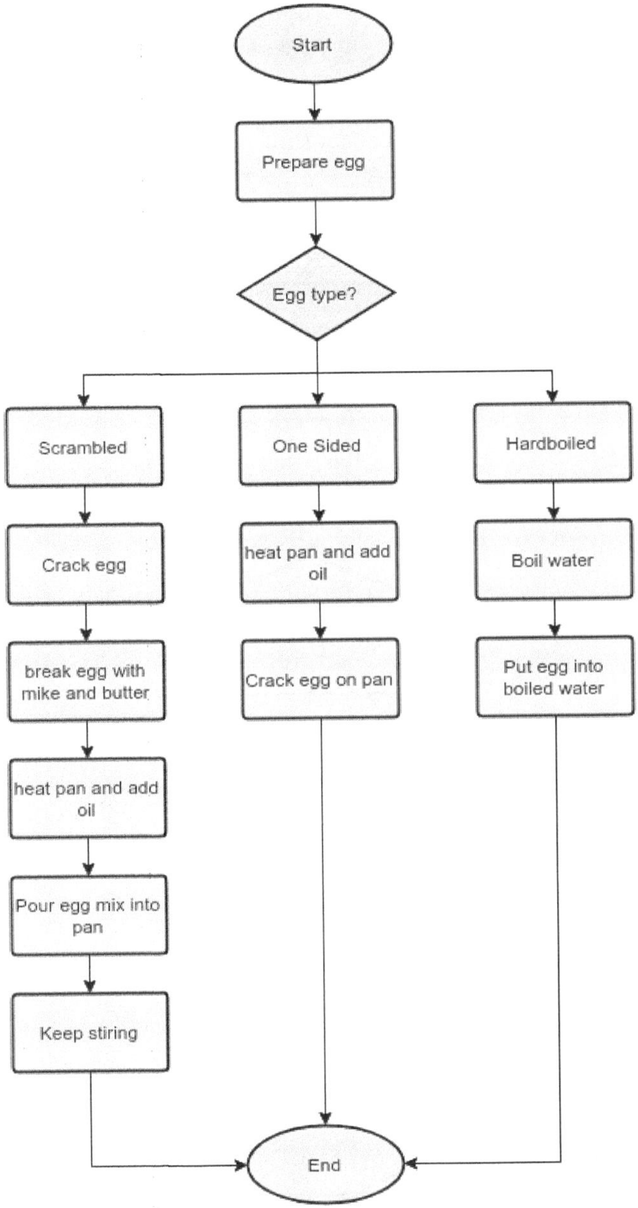
Start
Prepare egg
Egg type?
Scrambled
Crack egg
break egg with mike and butter
heat pan and add oil
Pour egg mix into pan
Keep stiring
One Sided
heat pan and add oil
Crack egg on pan
Hardboiled
Boil water
Put egg into boiled water
End

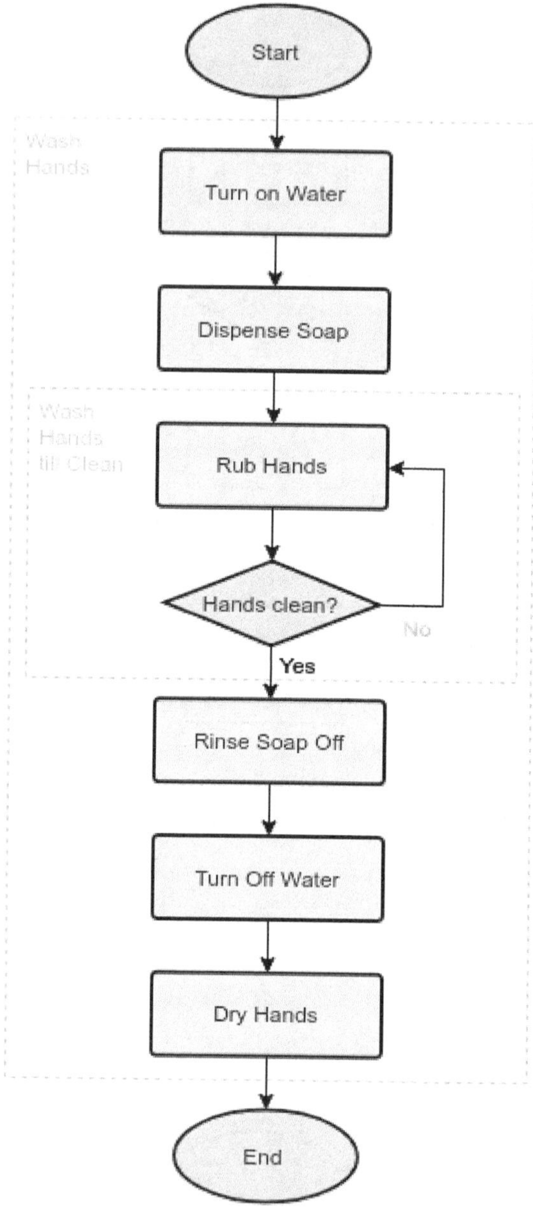
Start
Wash Hands
Turn on Water
Dispense Soap
Wash Hands till Clean
Rub Hands
Hands clean?
No
Yes
Rinse Soap Off
Turn Off Water
Dry Hands
End

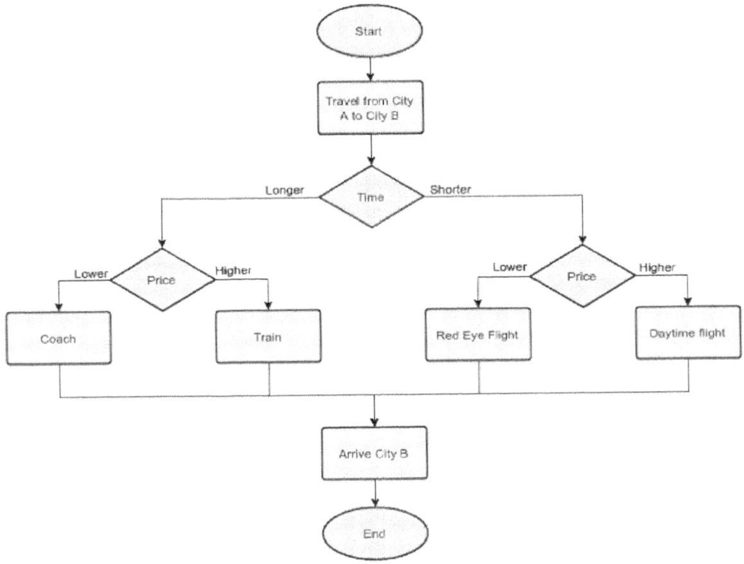
Start
Travel from City A to City B
Time
Longer
Shorter
Price
Lower
Higher
Coach
Train
Price
Lower
Higher
Red Eye Flight
Daytime flight
Arrive City B
End

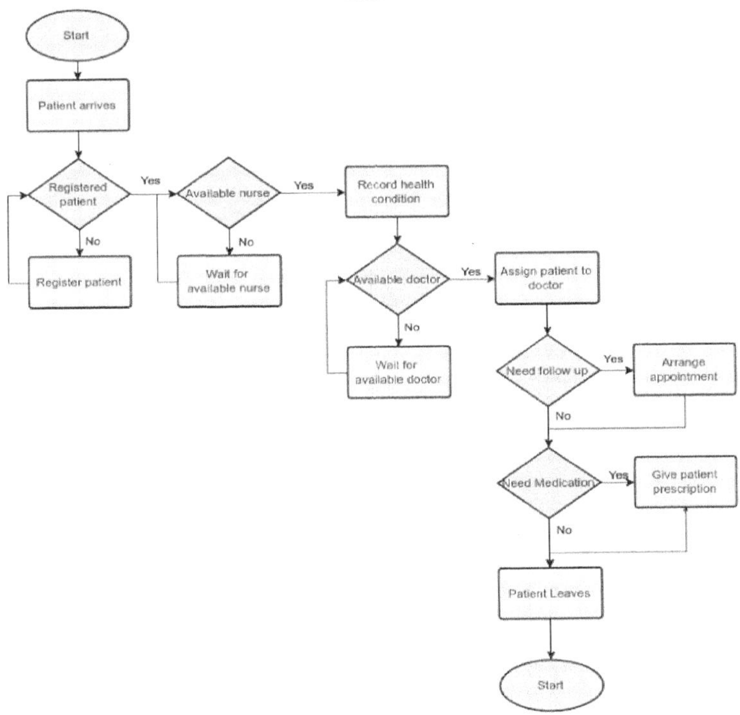
Start
Patient arrives
Registered patient
Yes
No
Register patient
Available nurse
Yes
No
Wait for available nurse
Record health condition
Available doctor
Yes
No
Wait for available doctor
Assign patient to doctor
Need follow up
Yes
No
Arrange appointment
Need Medication
Yes
No
Give patient prescription
Patient Leaves
Start

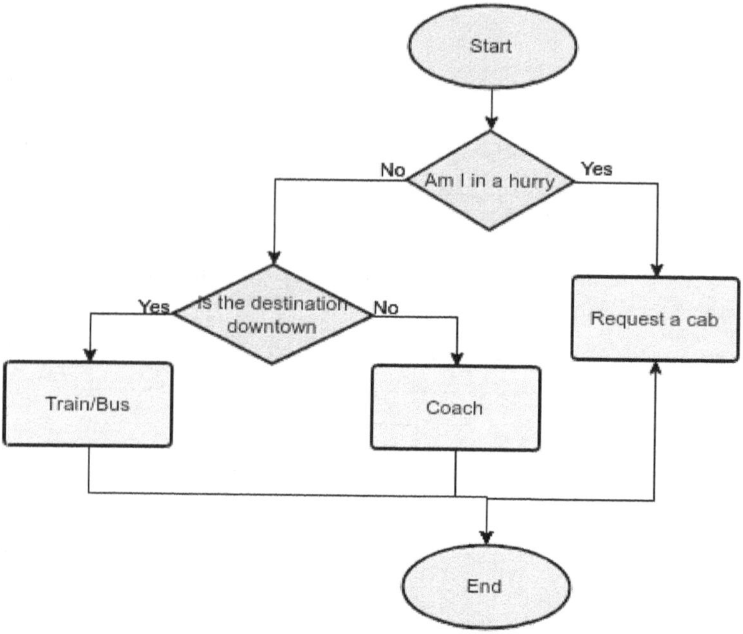
Start
Am I in a hurry
No
Yes
Is the destination downtown
Yes
No
Request a cab
Train/Bus
Coach
End

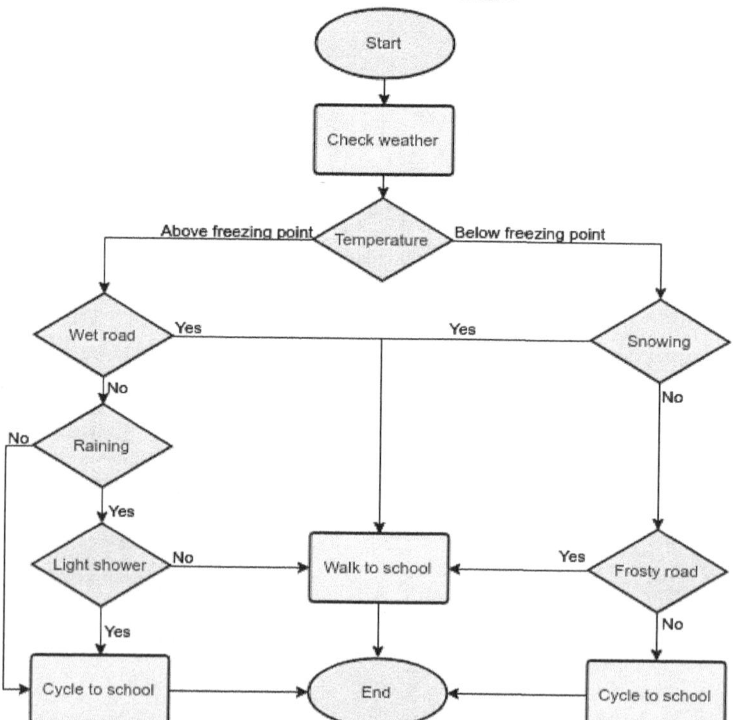
Start
Check weather
Temperature
Above freezing point
Below freezing point
Wet road
Yes
Yes
Snowing
No
No
Raining
No
Yes
Light shower
No
Walk to school
Yes
Frosty road
Yes
No
Cycle to school
End
Cycle to school

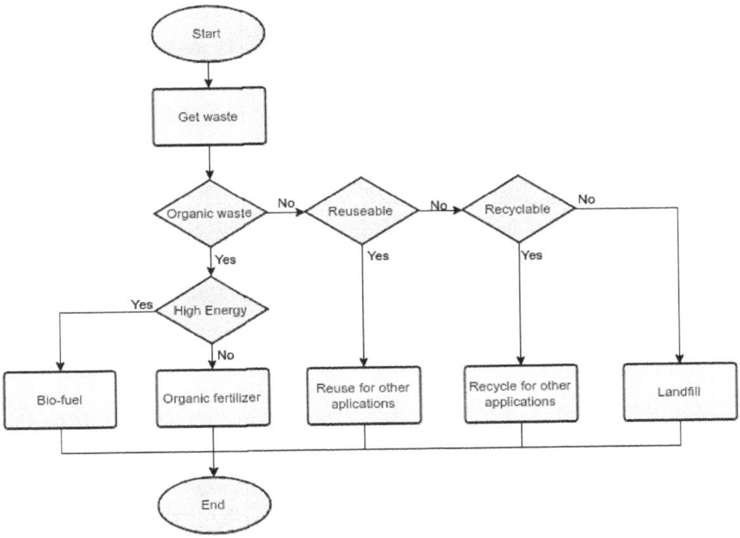
Start
Get waste
Organic waste
No
Reuseable
No
Recyclable
No
Yes
Yes
Yes
Yes
High Energy
No
Bio-fuel
Organic fertilizer
Reuse for other aplications
Recycle for other applications
Landfill
End

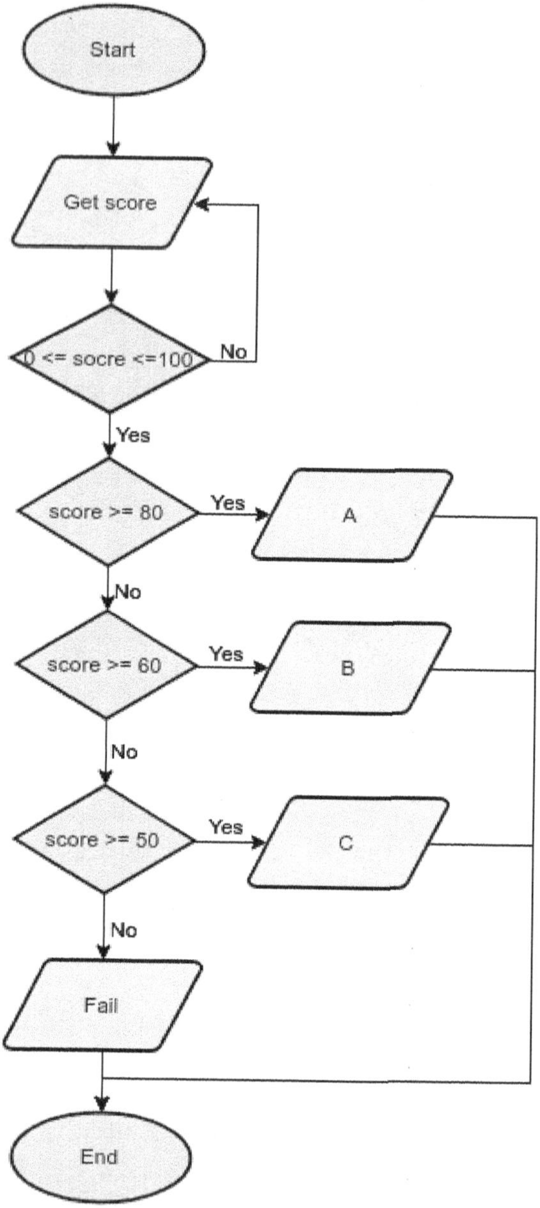
Start
Get score
0 <= socre <=100
No
Yes
score >= 80
Yes
A
No
score >= 60
Yes
B
No
score >= 50
Yes
C
No
Fail
End

LIST OF LAB EXPERIMENTS(EST 102 Programming in C Semester 2 APJ Kerala Technological Univ. LAB syllabus)

1. **Familiarization of Hardware Components of a Computer.**

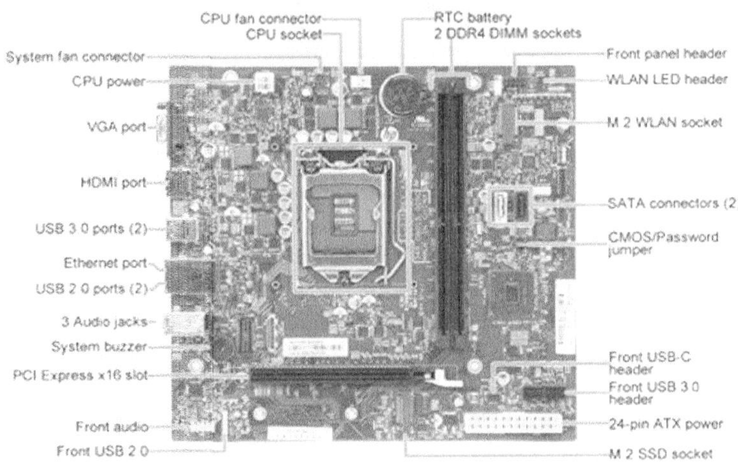

System Fan
Floppy
Heat Sink
Hard Drive
Power Supply
Optical Drive
Motherboard
Processors (CPU)
RAM Moduels

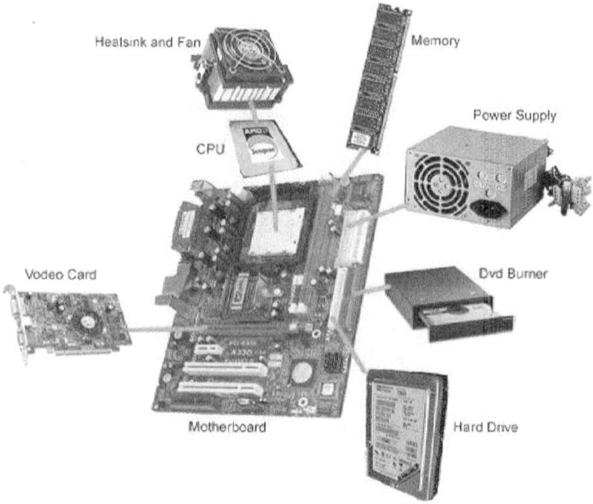
Heatsink and Fan
Memory
Power Supply
CPU
Vodeo Card
Dvd Burner
Motherboard
Hard Drive

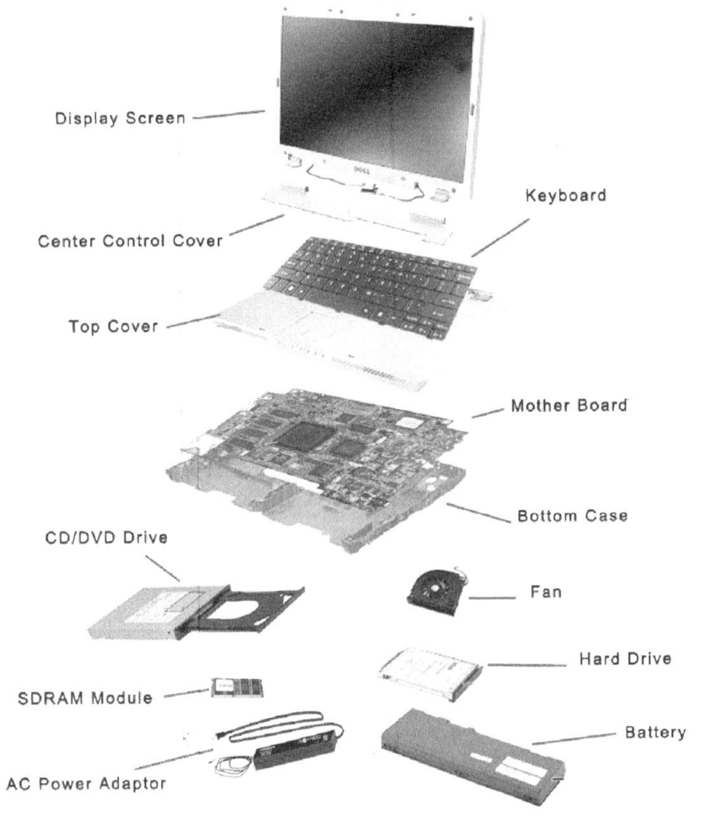
Display Screen
Keyboard
Center Control Cover
Top Cover
Mother Board
Bottom Case
CD/DVD Drive
Fan
Hard Drive
SDRAM Module
Battery
AC Power Adaptor

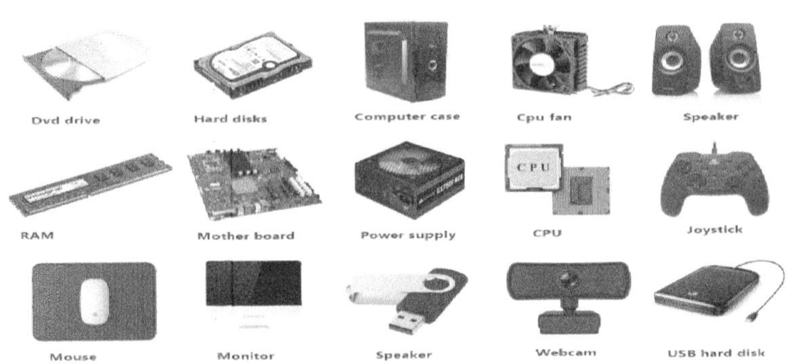
Dvd drive
Hard disks
Computer case
Cpu fan
Speaker
RAM
Mother board
Power supply
CPU
Joystick
Mouse
Monitor
Speaker
Webcam
USB hard disk

computer
monitor
case
motherboard
memory
mouse
speakers
CPU
key
keyboard
cable
chip
DVD
flash drive
hard drive
headphones
joystick
laptop
microphone
modem
tablet
webcam

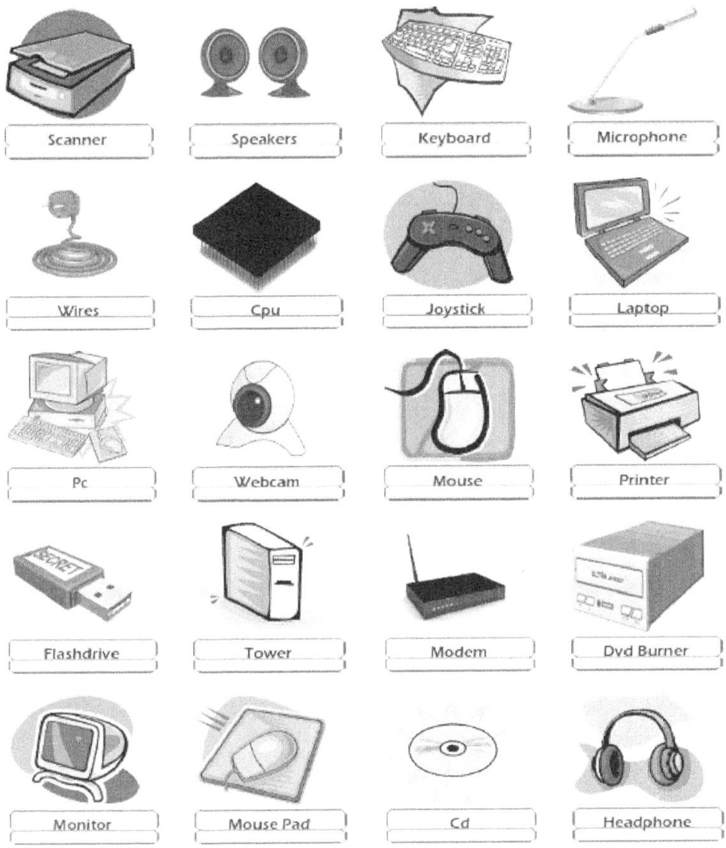
Scanner
Speakers
Keyboard
Microphone
Wires
Cpu
Joystick
Laptop
Pc
Webcam
Mouse
Printer
Flashdrive
Tower
Modem
Dvd Burner
Monitor
Mouse Pad
Cd
Headphone

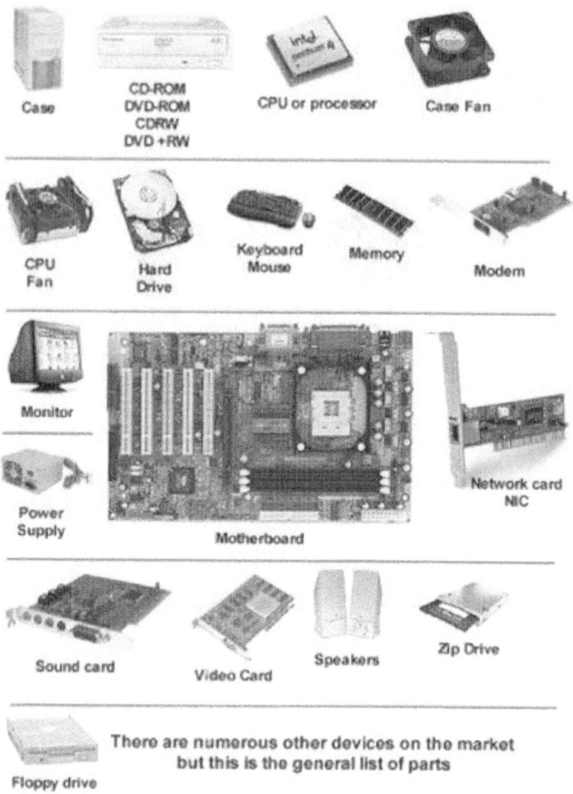
Case
CD-ROM
DVD-ROM
CDRW
DVD +RW
CPU or processor
Case Fan
CPU
Fan
Hard
Drive
Keyboard
Mouse
Memory
Modem
Monitor
Power
Supply
Motherboard
Network card
NIC
Sound card
Video Card
Speakers
Zip Drive
Floppy drive
There are numerous other devices on the market
but this is the general list of parts

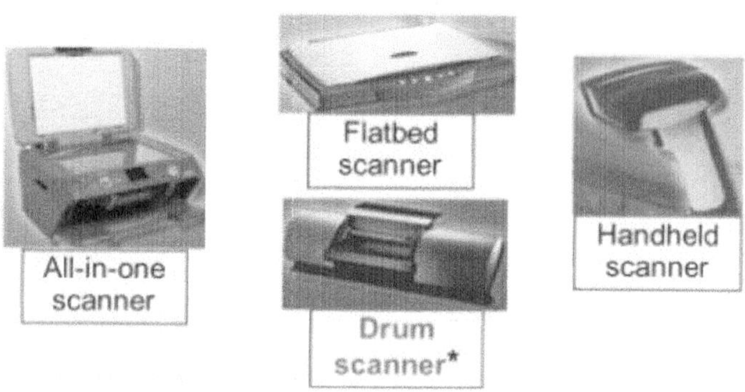
All-in-one
scanner
Flatbed
scanner
Drum
scanner*
Handheld
scanner

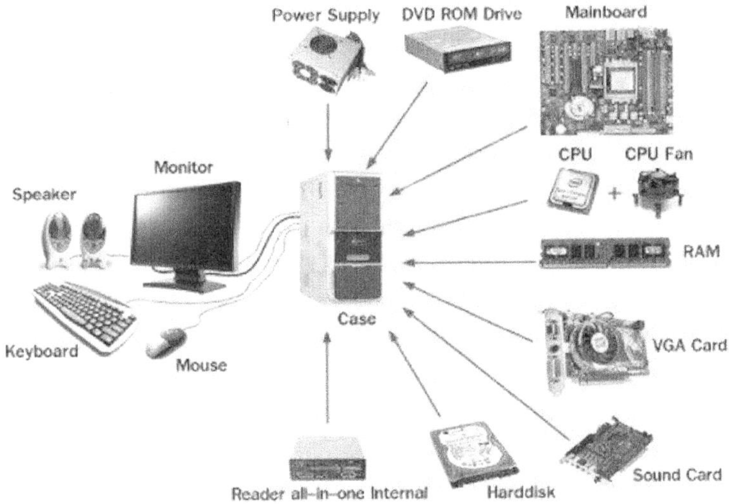
Power Supply
DVD ROM Drive
Mainboard
CPU
CPU Fan
RAM
VGA Card
Sound Card
Harddisk
Reader all-in-one Internal
Case
Monitor
Speaker
Keyboard
Mouse

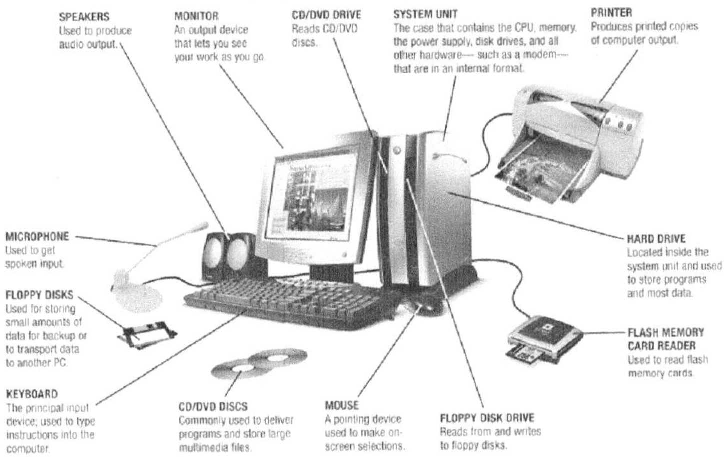
SPEAKERS
Used to produce audio output.
MONITOR
An output device that lets you see your work as you go.
CD/DVD DRIVE
Reads CD/DVD discs.
SYSTEM UNIT
The case that contains the CPU, memory, the power supply, disk drives, and all other hardware— such as a modem— that are in an internal format.
PRINTER
Produces printed copies of computer output.
MICROPHONE
Used to get spoken input.
HARD DRIVE
Located inside the system unit and used to store programs and most data.
FLOPPY DISKS
Used for storing small amounts of data for backup or to transport data to another PC.
FLASH MEMORY CARD READER
Used to read flash memory cards.
KEYBOARD
The principal input device; used to type instructions into the computer.
CD/DVD DISCS
Commonly used to deliver programs and store large multimedia files.
MOUSE
A pointing device used to make on-screen selections.
FLOPPY DISK DRIVE
Reads from and writes to floppy disks.

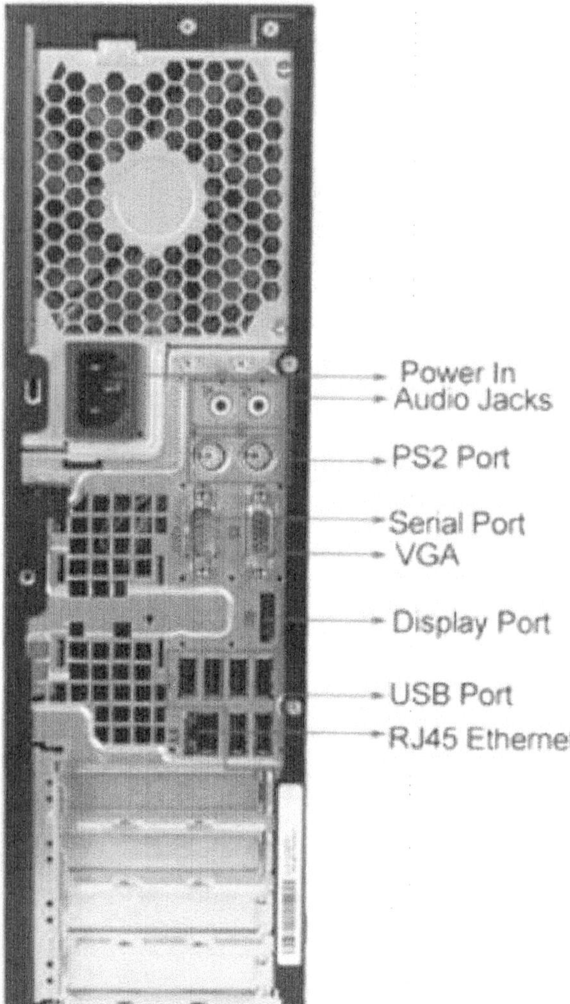
Power In
Audio Jacks
PS2 Port
Serial Port
VGA
Display Port
USB Port
RJ45 Ethernet

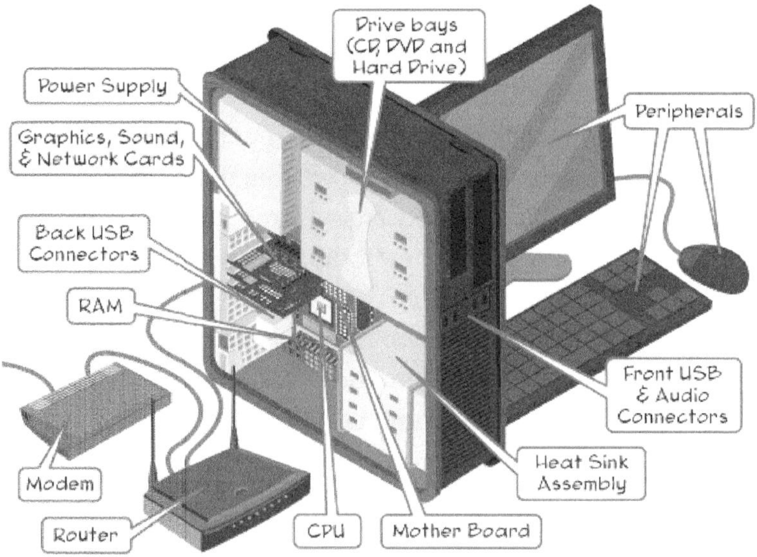

2. Familiarization of Linux environment – How to do Programming in C with Linux

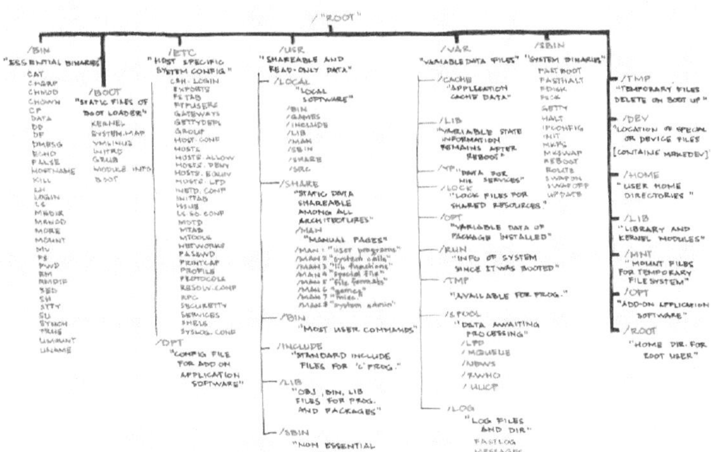

Join www.tryhackme.com

Try the following,

1. https://tryhackme.com/room/linuxfundamentalspart1
2. https://tryhackme.com/room/linuxfundamentalspart2
3. https://tryhackme.com/room/linuxfundamentalspart3
4. https://tryhackme.com/room/rrootme
5. https://tryhackme.com/room/linuxprivesc
6. https://tryhackme.com/room/introtoshells
7. https://tryhackme.com/room/commonlinuxprivesc
8. https://tryhackme.com/room/lazyadmin
9. https://tryhackme.com/room/cowboyhacker

'ls' command:

root@kali:~# man ls

```
root@LAPTOP-KHULM439: ~/arun
LS(1)                                           User Commands

NAME
       ls - list directory contents

SYNOPSIS
       ls [OPTION]... [FILE]...

DESCRIPTION
       List  information  about the FILEs (the current directory by default).
       -cftuvSUX nor --sort is specified.
```

To list the files and folders in your current working directory:

root@kali:~# ls

```
root@kali:~# ls
Desktop
root@kali:~#
```

To get more even details about all the files within the directory:

root@kali:~# ls –a

```
oot@LAPTOP-KHULM439:~# ls -a
   .bashrc      .profile  Desktop    Downloads  Pictures  Templates  c     socket
 . .motd_shown  .viminfo  Documents  Music      Public    Videos     snap
```

Present Working Directory Details:

root@kali:~# pwd

```
root@LAPTOP-KHULM439:~# pwd
/root
```

Change Directory(Move one folder to other):

root@kali:~# cd foldername

```
root@LAPTOP-KHULM439:~# mkdir arun
root@LAPTOP-KHULM439:~# cd arun
root@LAPTOP-KHULM439:~/arun# touch emptyfile
root@LAPTOP-KHULM439:~/arun# ls
emptyfile
root@LAPTOP-KHULM439:~/arun# pwd
/root/arun
root@LAPTOP-KHULM439:~/arun#
```

Touch will help to create empty files.

Mkdir will help to create new directory.

Move back to previous folder/directory:

root@kali:/media# cd ..

```
root@LAPTOP-KHULM439:~/arun# cd ..
root@LAPTOP-KHULM439:~# ls
Desktop  Documents  Downloads  Music  Pictures  Public  Templates  Videos  arun  c  snap  socket
```

Linux Text Editors: VI/VIM/GEDIT/NANO.

To see contents of the created file:

root@kali:~# cat sample.txt

```
root@LAPTOP-KHULM439:~# vi sample.txt
root@LAPTOP-KHULM439:~# cat sample.txt
it is sample
```

'vi' is a text editor. For inserting new data, you have to press 'i' or 'insert' button. Once data is added, you can press ESC button, then follow the steps,

1. :wq for saving & quit
2. :q! for not saving & quit.

Copy file contents and save that contents in other file: Suppose you are creating 'C program for addition'. Next program is 'C program for subtraction'. So you can copy 'add.c' into 'subtract', just change operator alone, you can see the subtraction results. Otherwise, you may have to write entire lines once again. You can save time by doing this.

root@kali:/# cp add.csubtract

```
root@LAPTOP-KHULM439:~# vi sum.c
root@LAPTOP-KHULM439:~# cp sum.c substract.c
root@LAPTOP-KHULM439:~# cat sum.c
#include<stdio.h>
root@LAPTOP-KHULM439:~# cat substract.c
#include<stdio.h>
```

Move this substract.c file to substract folder, then the following steps need to follow,

```
root@LAPTOP-KHULM439:~# mv substract.c /subtract/.
mv: cannot move 'substract.c' to '/subtract/.': No such file or directory
root@LAPTOP-KHULM439:~# mv substract.c subtract/.
root@LAPTOP-KHULM439:~# cd subtract/
root@LAPTOP-KHULM439:~/subtract# ls
substract.c
```

Delete File:

```
root@LAPTOP-KHULM439:~/subtract# touch for_delete
root@LAPTOP-KHULM439:~/subtract# ls
for_delete  substract.c
root@LAPTOP-KHULM439:~/subtract# rm for_delete
root@LAPTOP-KHULM439:~/subtract# ls
substract.c
```

Remove Directory:

```
root@LAPTOP-KHULM439:~/subtract# mkdir for_delete
root@LAPTOP-KHULM439:~/subtract# ls
for_delete  substract.c
root@LAPTOP-KHULM439:~/subtract# rmdir for_delete/
root@LAPTOP-KHULM439:~/subtract# ls
substract.c
```

You want to change mode(User to administrator(root) mode):

chmod +x filename.c

or

chmod 777 filename.c

```
-rw-r--r-- 1 root root 18 Jun  4 19:37 substract.c
root@LAPTOP-KHULM439:~/subtract# chmod +x substract.c
root@LAPTOP-KHULM439:~/subtract# ll
total 12
drwxr-xr-x 2 root root 4096 Jun  4 19:44 ./
drwx------ 8 root root 4096 Jun  4 19:39 ../
-rwxr-xr-x 1 root root   18 Jun  4 19:37 substract.c*
root@LAPTOP-KHULM439:~/subtract# vi add.c
root@LAPTOP-KHULM439:~/subtract# chmod 777 substract.c
root@LAPTOP-KHULM439:~/subtract# ll
total 16
drwxr-xr-x 2 root root 4096 Jun  4 19:46 ./
drwx------ 8 root root 4096 Jun  4 19:46 ../
-rw-r--r-- 1 root root   18 Jun  4 19:46 add.c
-rwxrwxrwx 1 root root   18 Jun  4 19:37 substract.c*
```

Both helped to add 'execute' option in that particular file. In linux, we normally give permissions to shell or perl scripts or c programs, before executing that files.

Update your Kali Linux software:

root@kali:/# sudo apt-get update

root@kali:/# sudo apt-get upgrade

To become system admin without having to use sudoeverytime:

root@kali:/# sudo –s

To change to super user mode, use 'su–'

To View Ip address of your machine:

root@kali:/# ifconfig

if 'ifconfig' not found, consider last line which was mentioned in the below figure.

```
root@LAPTOP-KHULM439:~/subtract# ifconfig
eth0: flags=4163<UP,BROADCAST,RUNNING,MULTICAST>  mtu 1500
        inet 172.29.72.236  netmask 255.255.240.0  broadcast 172.29.79.255
        inet6 fe80::215:5dff:fe34:ea7c  prefixlen 64  scopeid 0x20<link>
        ether 00:15:5d:34:ea:7c  txqueuelen 1000  (Ethernet)
        RX packets 407  bytes 267556 (267.5 KB)
        RX errors 0  dropped 0  overruns 0  frame 0
        TX packets 166  bytes 12493 (12.4 KB)
        TX errors 0  dropped 0 overruns 0  carrier 0  collisions 0

lo: flags=73<UP,LOOPBACK,RUNNING>  mtu 65536
        inet 127.0.0.1  netmask 255.0.0.0
        inet6 ::1  prefixlen 128  scopeid 0x10<host>
        loop  txqueuelen 1000  (Local Loopback)
        RX packets 0  bytes 0 (0.0 B)
        RX errors 0  dropped 0  overruns 0  frame 0
        TX packets 0  bytes 0 (0.0 B)
        TX errors 0  dropped 0 overruns 0  carrier 0  collisions 0

root@LAPTOP-KHULM439:~/subtract# apt install net-tools
```

Loop Back Address:

root@kali:~# ping 127.0.0.1

```
root@LAPTOP-KHULM439:~/subtract# ping 127.0.0.1
PING 127.0.0.1 (127.0.0.1) 56(84) bytes of data.
64 bytes from 127.0.0.1: icmp_seq=1 ttl=64 time=0.139 ms
64 bytes from 127.0.0.1: icmp_seq=2 ttl=64 time=0.044 ms
64 bytes from 127.0.0.1: icmp_seq=3 ttl=64 time=0.047 ms
64 bytes from 127.0.0.1: icmp_seq=4 ttl=64 time=0.062 ms
```

Setup New use account:

```
root@LAPTOP-KHULM439:~/subtract# adduser arunanoopm
Adding user `arunanoopm' ...
Adding new group `arunanoopm' (1002) ...
Adding new user `arunanoopm' (1002) with group `arunanoopm' ...
Creating home directory `/home/arunanoopm' ...
Copying files from `/etc/skel' ...
New password:
Retype new password:
passwd: password updated successfully
Changing the user information for arunanoopm
Enter the new value, or press ENTER for the default
        Full Name []: Dr.Arun_Anoop_M
        Room Number []: 212
        Work Phone []: 9497394076
        Home Phone []:
        Other []:
Is the information correct? [Y/n] Y
root@LAPTOP-KHULM439:~/subtract#
```

If it's windows10, press windows button (keyboard). Type 'microsoft store' then type 'ubuntu'. Select Ubuntu 22.04 LTS. Click on "GET" option. Once downloaded click on "OPEN" button. It will redirect ubuntu command prompt. It's WSL version of Ubuntu(Win+R button, command or cmd then type wsl –install)

To change password of normal user

Type sudo passwd

You can type your password. Whatever you are typing, it will not show anything. Keep on typing.

Change to admin mode. That's super mode. For super mode, you can type su – and press Enter button.

In order to compile and execute a C program, you need essential packages installed on your system. Enter the following command as root in your Linux Terminal:

$ sudo apt-get install build-essential

After installing the essential packages, let us write a simple C program.

Open Ubuntu's graphical Text Editor and write or copy the following sample program into it:

```
#include<stdio.h>
int main()
{
printf("\n Hello World\n\n");
return 0;
}
```

Then save the file with .c extension. In this example, I am naming my C program as Sample.c

Alternatively, you can write the C program through the Terminal in gedit as follows:

$ geditSample.c

This will create a .c file where you can write and save a program.

In your Terminal, enter the following command in order to make an executable version of the program you have written:

Syntax:

$ gcc [programName].c -o programName
$ gccSample.c -o Sample then type ./Sample
ORgccfilename.c then type ./a.out

The final step is to run the compiled C program. Use the following syntax to do so:

$ ./programName

Example:

$ ./Sample

You can see how the program is executed in the above example, displaying the text we wrote to print through it.

3. Familiarization of console I/O and operators in C

i) Display "Hello World"

Open vi sample.c

Press INSERT (Press keyboard 'I' letter)button in your keyboard.

arun@LAPTOP-KHULM439: ~

```
#include<stdio.h>

    int main()
        printf("Hello World");
    return 0;

~
```

Press ESCAPE button ESC

Then type :wq that means, write and quit

If you are not going to save it, you can type :!q

```
arun@LAPTOP-KHULM439:~$ gcc sample.c -o sample
```

```
arun@LAPTOP-KHULM439:~$ gcc sample.c -o sample
sample.c:2:1: error: expected identifier or '(' before '{' token
    2 | {
      | ^
arun@LAPTOP-KHULM439:~$ vi sample.c
```

arun@LAPTOP-KHULM439: ~

```
#include<stdio.h>
    int main()

    printf("Hello World");
    return 0;

~
~
~
```

```
arun@LAPTOP-KHULM439:~$ gcc sample.c -o sample
```

```
arun@LAPTOP-KHULM439:~$ vi sample.c
arun@LAPTOP-KHULM439:~$ gcc sample.c -o sample
arun@LAPTOP-KHULM439:~$
```

```
arun@LAPTOP-KHULM439:~$ gcc sample.c -o sample
arun@LAPTOP-KHULM439:~$ ./sample
Hello Worldarun@LAPTOP-KHULM439:~$
```

If I want to print the command line in next line, I can redit the above code.

arun@LAPTOP-KHULM439: ~

```
#include<stdio.h>
        int main()
{
        printf("Hello World\n");
        return 0;
}
~
```

```
arun@LAPTOP-KHULM439:~$ gcc sample.c -o sample
arun@LAPTOP-KHULM439:~$ ./sample
Hello World
arun@LAPTOP-KHULM439:~$
```

ii) Read two numbers, add them and display theirsum

arun@LAPTOP-KHULM439: ~

```
#include<stdio.h>
void main()
{
        int a,b,c;
        printf("Give your first number:");
        scanf("%d",&a);
        printf("Give your second number:");
        scanf("%d",&b);
        c=a+b;
        printf("Result=%d",c);
}
~
~
```

```
arun@LAPTOP-KHULM439:~$ vi add.c
arun@LAPTOP-KHULM439:~$ gcc add.c -o add
arun@LAPTOP-KHULM439:~$ ./add
Give your first number:2
Give your second number:3
Result=5arun@LAPTOP-KHULM439:~$ vi add.c
arun@LAPTOP-KHULM439:~$
```

arun@LAPTOP-KHULM439: ~

```
#include<stdio.h>
void main()
{
        int a,b,c;
        printf("Give your first number:");
        scanf("%d",&a);
        printf("Give your second number:");
        scanf("%d",&b);
        c=a+b;
        printf("Result=%d\n",c);
}
~
```

```
arun@LAPTOP-KHULM439:~$ vi add.c
arun@LAPTOP-KHULM439:~$ gcc add.c -o add
arun@LAPTOP-KHULM439:~$ ./add
Give your first number:4
Give your second number:3
Result=7
arun@LAPTOP-KHULM439:~$ vi add.c
arun@LAPTOP-KHULM439:~$
```

iii) Read the radius of a circle, calculate its area and display it

arun@LAPTOP-KHULM439: ~

```
#include<stdio.h>
void main()
{
        int r,area;
        printf("Enter radius:");
        scanf("%d",&r);
        area=3.14*r*r;
        printf("Area of circle is = %d\n",area);
}
~
```

```
arun@LAPTOP-KHULM439:~$ vi circle.c
arun@LAPTOP-KHULM439:~$ gcc circle.c -o circle
arun@LAPTOP-KHULM439:~$ ./circle
Enter radius:2
Area of circle is = 12
arun@LAPTOP-KHULM439:~$ vi circle.c
arun@LAPTOP-KHULM439:~$
```

3. **14 *4 is not 12. So we need to declare area as float, so that, it will display the correct results. Let us try for that.**

```
arun@LAPTOP-KHULM439: ~
#include<stdio.h>
#define pi 3.14
void main()
{
        int r;
        float area;
        printf("Enter radius:");
        scanf("%d",&r);
        area=pi*r*r;
        printf("Area of circle is = %f\n",area);
}

/* This is Another way */
```

```
arun@LAPTOP-KHULM439: ~
#include<stdio.h>
void main()
{
        int r;
        float area;
        printf("Enter radius:");
        scanf("%d",&r);
        area=3.14*r*r;
        printf("Area of circle is = %f\n",area);
}
~
~
~
```

```
arun@LAPTOP-KHULM439:~$ vi circle.c
arun@LAPTOP-KHULM439:~$ gcc circle.c -o circle
arun@LAPTOP-KHULM439:~$ ./circle
Enter radius:2
Area of circle is = 12.560000
arun@LAPTOP-KHULM439:~$ vi circle.c
arun@LAPTOP-KHULM439:~$
```

iv) Evaluate the arithmetic expression ((a -b / c * d + e) * (f +g)) and display its solution.Readthe values of the variables from the user through console.

arun@LAPTOP-KHULM439: ~

```
#include<stdio.h>
void main()
{
        int a,b,c,d,e,f,g,output;
        printf("Enter seven values\n");
        printf("==================\n");
        scanf("%d%d%d%d%d%d%d",&a,&b,&c,&d,&e,&f,&g);
        output=((a-b/c*d+e)*(f+g));
        printf("%d\n",output);
}
~
```

```
arun@LAPTOP-KHULM439:~$ vi arith.c
arun@LAPTOP-KHULM439:~$ gcc arith.c -o arith
arun@LAPTOP-KHULM439:~$ ./arith
Enter seven values
==================
1
2
1
1
1
1
1
0
arun@LAPTOP-KHULM439:~$ ./arith
Enter seven values
==================
4
2
2
1
3
1
1
12
```

1. **Read 3 integer values and find the largest among them.**

root@LAPTOP-KHULM439: ~/c

```
#include<stdio.h>
/* Dr.Arun Anoop M*/
void main()
{
        int num1,num2,num3;
        printf("Enter three numbers\n");
        scanf("%d%d%d",&num1,&num2,&num3);
        if(num1>num2)
        {
                printf("%d is greater\n",num1);
        }
        else if(num2>num3)
        {
                printf("%d is greater\n",num2);
        }
        else
        {
                printf("%d is greater\n",num3);
        }
}
~
```

```
root@LAPTOP-KHULM439:~/c# vi threei.c
root@LAPTOP-KHULM439:~/c# gcc threei.c -o threei
root@LAPTOP-KHULM439:~/c# ./threei
Enter three numbers
3
4
2
4 is greater
```

2. Read a Natural Number and check whether the number is prime or not

Concept:
Number which is having 2 factors.
Suppose n=7
Variable 'i' carrying 1 to 7
If any factor(divisible or not) found increase the count value(Set count=0 initially during variable declaration.)
'i' represent in a loop upto n.
If count equal to 2 , then it is a prime number.

root@LAPTOP-KHULM439: ~/c

```
#include<stdio.h>
/* Dr.Arun Anoop M*/
void main()
{
        int num,i,c=0;
        printf("Enter the number:");
        scanf("%d",&num);
        for(i=1;i<=num;i++)
        {
                if(num%i==0)
                {
                        c++;
                }
        }
        if(c==2)
        {
                printf("%d is prime\n",num);
        }
        else
        {
                printf("%d is not prime\n",num);
        }
}
```

```
root@LAPTOP-KHULM439:~/c# vi prime.c
root@LAPTOP-KHULM439:~/c# gcc prime.c -o prime
root@LAPTOP-KHULM439:~/c# ./prime
Enter the number:4
4 is not primeroot@LAPTOP-KHULM439:~/c# ./prime
Enter the number:1
1 is not primeroot@LAPTOP-KHULM439:~/c# ./prime
Enter the number:2
2 is primeroot@LAPTOP-KHULM439:~/c#
```

3. **Read a Natural Number and check whether the number is Armstrong or not**

Concept:

Sum of cube of each digits must be equal to the same number.

Example: $153=1^3+5^3+3^3=1+125+27=153$

1. While loop for checking the given number is greater than 0.
2. Find the digits one by one and storing it into a variable. We know that container jeep is for storing mud. Likewise, here we have variable concept to store values for calculation.
3. Digits one by one we can collect by the help of modulus operator. And output we can store to new variable.
4. Now as per example we got 1,5,3 digits. Now next process will be cube finding steps. Output we will store into new variable.
5. Next step is for addition process. Already sum initially as zero. So that sum we will add with the cube of each digits.
6. Next we need to take rest of the digits by the help of division operation. So num variable value will be changed by new one.

7. Next will check the final output is equal to number we selected for checking. If yes, its Armstrong number else not an Armstrong number.

root@LAPTOP-KHULM439: ~/c

```
#include<stdio.h>
/*Dr.Arun Anoop M*/
void main()
{
        int num,sum=0,reminder,count;
        printf("Enter the number:");
        scanf("%d",&num);
        while(num>0)
        {
                reminder=num%10;
                count=reminder*reminder*reminder;
                sum=sum+count;
                num=num/10;
        }

        if(sum==num)
        {
                printf("%d is armstrong number\n",num);
        }
        else
        {
                printf("%d is not an armstrong number\n",num);
        }
}
~
~
```

```
root@LAPTOP-KHULM439:~/c# vi arms.c
root@LAPTOP-KHULM439:~/c# gcc arms.c -o arms
root@LAPTOP-KHULM439:~/c# ./arms
Enter the number:153
0 is not an armstrong number
```

Okey let me use temp variable to avoid these problems.

root@LAPTOP-KHULM439: ~/c

```
#include<stdio.h>
/* Dr.Arun Anoop M*/
void main()
{
        int num,sum=0,reminder,count,temp;
        printf("Enter the number:");
        scanf("%d",&num);
        temp=num;
        while(num>0)
        {
                reminder=num%10;
                count=reminder*reminder*reminder;
                sum=sum+count;
                num=num/10;
        }
        num=temp;
        if(sum==num)
        {
                printf("%d is armstrong number\n",num);
        }
        else
        {
                printf("%d is not an armstrong number\n",num);
        }
}
```

```
root@LAPTOP-KHULM439:~/c# vi arms1.c
root@LAPTOP-KHULM439:~/c# gcc arms1.c -o arms1
root@LAPTOP-KHULM439:~/c# ./arms1
Enter the number:153
153 is armstrong number
```

Next important questions area) WAP to check palindrome number b) WAP to Print Fibonacci series of number c) WAP to check reverse of a number.

Before moving to university lab questions, let me add the above question's codes.

Write a Program to find reverse of a number.

1. Identify its digits by the help of modulus operation.&check given number is greater than zero.
2. Use the equation 'sum*10+reminder' and stored it in location of sum variable.
   sum=sum*10+reminder (sum initialized as zero at the time of variable declaration).

3. Rest of the digits need to process next with the help of division operator and store the output into given number stored variable.

root@LAPTOP-KHULM439: ~/c

```
#include<stdio.h>
/* Dr.Arun ANoop M*/
void main()
{
        int num,sum=0,reminder;
        printf("Enter the number:");
        scanf("%d",&num);
        while(num>0)
        {
                reminder=num%10;
                sum=sum*10+reminder;
                num=num/10;
        }
        printf("Reversed value of given number is= %d\n",sum);
}
```

```
root@LAPTOP-KHULM439:~/c# vi reves.c
root@LAPTOP-KHULM439:~/c# gcc reves.c -o reves
root@LAPTOP-KHULM439:~/c# ./reves
Enter the number:1256
Reversed value of given number is= 6521
```

Write a Program to find Palindrome of a Number.

1. Same as reverse of a number.
2. Check given number is equal to sum variable.
3. It will give u results.

root@LAPTOP-KHULM439: ~/c

```
#include<stdio.h>
/* Dr Arun ANoop M*/
void main()
{
        int num,sum=0,reminder;
        printf("Enter the number:");
        scanf("%d",&num);
        while(num>0)
        {
                reminder=num%10;
                sum=sum*10+reminder;
                num=num/10;
        }
        if(num==sum)
        {
                printf("%d is a Palindrome number\n",num);
        }
        else
        {
                printf("%d is not a Palindrome number\n",num);
        }
}
```

```
root@LAPTOP-KHULM439:~/c# vi palind.c
root@LAPTOP-KHULM439:~/c# gcc palind.c -o palind
root@LAPTOP-KHULM439:~/c# ./palind
Enter the number:5225
0 is not a Palindrome number
```

Okey will add temp variable to avoid this.

root@LAPTOP-KHULM439: ~/c

```
#include<stdio.h>
/*Dr.Arun ANoop M*/
void main()
{
        int num,temp,sum=0,reminder;
        printf("Enter the number:");
        scanf("%d",&num);
        temp=num;
        while(num>0)
        {
                reminder=num%10;
                sum=sum*10+reminder;
                num=num/10;
        }
        num=temp;
        if(num==sum)
        {
                printf("%d is a Palindrome number\n",num);
        }
        else
        {
                printf("%d is not a Palindrome number\n",num);
        }
}
```

```
root@LAPTOP-KHULM439:~/c# vi palind.c
root@LAPTOP-KHULM439:~/c# gcc palind.c -o palind
root@LAPTOP-KHULM439:~/c# ./palind
Enter the number:2332
2332 is a Palindrome number
```

Write a Program to Print Fibonacci series:

Fibonacci Series: 0,1,1,2,3,….. (0+1=1;1+1=2;1+2=3,..)

Add a & b and value store in to c.

a=0, b=1, c=0+1=1.

a   <= b   <= c

b value we are storing into a& c value we are storing in to b.

```
root@LAPTOP-KHULM439: ~/c

#include<stdio.h>
/* Dr.Arun Anoop M*/

void main()
{
        int i,n,a=0,b=1,c;
        printf("Enter the limit");
        scanf("%d",&n);
        for(i=1;i<=n;i++)
        {
                printf("%d\n",a);
                c=a+b;
                a=b;
                b=c;
        }
}
```

```
root@LAPTOP-KHULM439:~/c# vi fibo.c
root@LAPTOP-KHULM439:~/c# gcc fibo.c -o fibo
root@LAPTOP-KHULM439:~/c# ./fibo
Enter the limit5
0
1
1
2
3
```

4. Read n integers, store them in an array and find their sum and average

Array is the collection of same data type of values that share a common name.

An uninitialized array is created as follows:

```
datatype arr[array_size];
Example: int a[10];
```

Accessing Array Elements as follows:

```
arr[idx];
```

The first and last elements in the array can be found at the following indices:

```
firstElement = arr[0];
lastElement = arr[arraySize - 1];
```

Assigning values to Array:

1. Initialization
   int salary[3]={10000,15000,30000}
   Array Index 0 1 2
2. Normal Assignment
   int sal[3];
   sal[0]=10000;
   sal[1]=15000;
   sal[2]=30000;
3. RunTime Assignment
   int sal[3];
   printf("Enter three employees salary\n");
   for(i=0;i<5;i++)
   {
   scanf("%d",&sal[i]);
   }
   Display salary:
   Same above code

Then

```
for(i=0;i<5;i++)
{
printf("Employees salary=%d\n",sal[i]);
}
```

root@LAPTOP-KHULM439: ~/c

```
#include<stdio.h>
/* Dr.Arun Anoop M */
void main()
{
        int i,sal[3];
        printf("Enter employees salary:\n");
        for(i=0;i<3;i++)
        {
                scanf("%d",&sal[i]);
        }
        for(i=0;i<3;i++)
        {
                printf("Employees's salary=%d",sal[i]);
        }
}
```

root@LAPTOP-KHULM439: ~/c

```
array.c:8:29: error: 'al' undeclared (first use in this function); did you mean 'sal'?
    8 |                 scanf("%d",&al[i]);
      |                             ^~
      |                             sal
root@LAPTOP-KHULM439:~/c# vi array.c
root@LAPTOP-KHULM439:~/c# gcc array.c -o array
array.c: In function 'main':
array.c:6:13: error: 'i' undeclared (first use in this function)
    6 |         for(i=0;i<5;i++)
      |             ^
array.c:6:13: note: each undeclared identifier is reported only once for each function it appears in
root@LAPTOP-KHULM439:~/c# vi array.c
root@LAPTOP-KHULM439:~/c# gcc array.c -o array
root@LAPTOP-KHULM439:~/c# ./array
Enter employees salary:
10
20
11
22
12
*** stack smashing detected ***: terminated
Aborted
root@LAPTOP-KHULM439:~/c# vi array.c
root@LAPTOP-KHULM439:~/c# gcc array.c -o array
root@LAPTOP-KHULM439:~/c# ./array
Enter employees salary:
10000
12000
15000
```

```
root@LAPTOP-KHULM439:~/c# ./array
Enter employees salary:
10000
12000
13000
Employees's salary=10000Employees's salary=12000Employees's salary=13000r
root@LAPTOP-KHULM439:~/c#
```

1st error: Missed to add ‘s’

2nd error: variable ‘i’ not declared.

3rd error: Initized sal[3] but mentioned ‘i<5’. Size is only 3, but we added 5 elements.

4th option: printf(“Employee %d salary=%d\n”, i,sal[i]);

root@LAPTOP-KHULM439: ~/c

```
#include<stdio.h>
/* Dr.Arun Anoop M */
void main()
{
        int i,sal[3];
        printf("Enter employees salary:\n");
        for(i=0;i<3;i++)
        {
                scanf("%d",&sal[i]);
        }
        for(i=0;i<3;i++)
        {
                printf("Employees %d's salary=%d\n",i,sal[i]);
        }
}
```

```
39:~/c# vi array.c
root@LAPTOP-KHULM439:~/c# gcc array.c -o array
root@LAPTOP-KHULM439:~/c# ./array
Enter employees salary:
120000
230000
400000
Employees 0's salary=120000
Employees 1's salary=230000
Employees 2's salary=400000
```

root@LAPTOP-KHULM439: ~/c

```
#include<stdio.h>
/* Dr.Arun Anoop M*/
void main()
{
        int i,n,sum=0,a[100];
        printf("Enter the limit:\n");
        scanf("%d",&n);
        printf("Enter the elements:\n");
        for(i=0;i<n;i++)
        {
                scanf("%d",&a[n]);
                sum=sum+a[n];
        }
        printf("Sum=%d\n",sum);
}
```

```
root@LAPTOP-KHULM439:~/c# ./sarray
Enter the limit:
4
Enter the elements:
2
3
1
2
Sum=8
```

root@LAPTOP-KHULM439: ~/c

```
#include<stdio.h>
/* Dr.Arun Anoop M*/
void main()
{
        int i,n,sum=0,a[100],avg=0;
        printf("Enter the limit:\n");
        scanf("%d",&n);
        printf("Enter the elements:\n");
        for(i=0;i<n;i++)
        {
                scanf("%d",&a[n]);
                sum=sum+a[n];
                avg=sum/n;
        }
        printf("Sum=%d\n",sum);
        printf("Average=%d\n",avg);
}
```

```
root@LAPTOP-KHULM439:~/c# vi avgarray.c
root@LAPTOP-KHULM439:~/c# ./avgarray
Enter the limit:
5
Enter the elements:
3
2
4
1
0
Sum=10
Average=2
```

5. Read n integers, store them in an array and search for an element in thearray using an algorithm for Linear Search

Concept:

1. /* Dr.Arun Anoop M */ This algorithm will help you to write program. Concept wise you must be strong.
2. Enter the limit and read the value.

3. Enter elements.
4. Read array.
5. Declare key element to search in the element list.
6. Denote key element as 'temp'.
7. Go to variable initialization step then assign k=0.
8. Open for loop.
9. If temp value == array index corresponding value, then increment 'k' value.
10. If k=0 , then "element not found". Else "element found".

root@LAPTOP-KHULM439: ~/c

```
#include<stdio.h>
/* Dr.Arun Anoop M*/
void main()
{
        int a[100],i,k=0,temp,n;
        printf("Enter the limit:\n");
        scanf("%d",&n);
        printf("Enter the elements:\n");
        for(i=0;i<n;i++)
        {
                scanf("%d",&a[i]);
        }
        printf("Enter the element to search:\n");
        scanf("%d",&temp);
        for(i=0;i<n;i++)
        {
        if(temp==a[i])
        {
                k+=1;

        }
        }
        if(k==0)
        {
                printf("Element not found\n");
        }
        else
        {
                printf("Element Found\n");
        }
}
```

```
root@LAPTOP-KHULM439:~/c# vi lsearch.c
root@LAPTOP-KHULM439:~/c# gcc lsearch.c -o lsearch
root@LAPTOP-KHULM439:~/c# ./lsearch
Enter the limit:
5
Enter the elements:
3
2
4
5
1
Enter the element to search:
5
Element Found
root@LAPTOP-KHULM439:~/c# ./lsearch
Enter the limit:
5
Enter the elements:
4
3
5
6
1
Enter the element to search:
7
Element not found
```

6. Read n integers, store them in an array and sort the elements in the array using Bubble Sortalgorithm

Concept:

1. /* Dr.Arun Anoop M */ This algorithm will help you to write program. Concept wise you must be strong.
2. Enter the limit and read the value.
3. Enter elements.
4. For loop to Read array.
5. Accessing array elements to sort
   5.1 i=0 uptolimit 'n'.
   5.2 j=i+1 uptolimit 'n'.
   5.3 Compare a[i] &a[j] by the help of greater operator.
6. Swapping elements
   6.1 First array output move to temp variable.
   6.2 Second array output move to first.
   6.3 Temp output move to Second array.

7. For loop to Print sorted array.

root@LAPTOP-KHULM439: ~/c

```
#include<stdio.h>
/* Dr.Arun Anoop M */
void main()
{
        int i,j,n,temp,a[100];
        printf("Enter the limit:\n");
        scanf("%d",&n);
        printf("Enter the elements:\n");
        for(i=0;i<n;i++)
        {
                scanf("%d",&a[i]);
        }
        for(i=0;i<n;i++)
        {
                for(j=i+1;j<n;j++)
                {
                        if(a[i]>a[j])
                        {
                                temp=a[i];
                                a[i]=a[j];
                                a[j]=temp;
                        }
                }
        }
        printf("Sorted Array is:\n");
        for(i=0;i<n;i++)
        {

                printf("%d\n",a[i]);
        }
}
```

```
root@LAPTOP-KHULM439:~/c# gcc bsort.c -o bsort
root@LAPTOP-KHULM439:~/c# ./bsort
Enter the limit:
5
Enter the elements:
12
45
55
67
32
Sorted Array is:
12
32
45
55
67
```

7. Read a string (word), store it in an array and check whether it is a palindrome word or not.

Concept:

1. /* Dr.Arun Anoop M */ This algorithm will help you to write program easily. Concept wise you must be strong.
2. Declare array to occupy string(data type is char), length to find string length, flag variable set to 0 initially. Declare string.h header file also.
3. Enter and read a string.
4. Identify the length of string by using string length in bult equation 'strlen'.
5. Store that string length in 'length' variable.
6. For loop of 'i' upto length of string.
   6.1 Compare string array & string array-i-1 by the help of 'not equal to' operator.
   6.2 Set flag equal to 1 and break the process.
   6.3 Close for loop.
7. If flag then string 's' is not a 'Palindrome'.
8. Else it is 'Palindrome'.

root@LAPTOP-KHULM439: ~/c

```
#include<stdio.h>
#include<string.h>
/* Dr.Arun Anoop M */
void main()
{
        int i,flag=0,length;
        char s[100];
        printf("Enter a string\n");
        scanf("%s",s);
        length=strlen(s);
        for(i=0;i<length;i++)
        {
                if(s[i]!=s[length-i-1])
                {
                        flag=1;
                        break;
                }
        }
                if(flag)
                {
                        printf("%s is not Palindrome\n",s);
                }
                else
                {
                        printf("%s is Palindrome\n",s);
                }

}
"palstring.c" 29L, 370B written
```

```
root@LAPTOP-KHULM439:~/c# vi palstring.c
root@LAPTOP-KHULM439:~/c# gcc palstring.c -o palstring
root@LAPTOP-KHULM439:~/c# ./palstring
Enter a string
PAAP
PAAP is Palindrome
```

8. Read two strings (each one ending with a $ symbol), store them inarrays and concatenate them without using library functions.

Concept:

1. /* Dr.Arun Anoop M */ This algorithm will help you to write program easily. Concept wise you must be strong.
2. Declare header files(Standard input output and string).
3. Enter First string and read it.
4. Identify its length by using 'strlen' and store into variable 'm'.

5. Enter Second string and read it.
6. Identify its length by using ‘strlen’ and store into new variable ‘n’.
7. For loop for ‘i’ and ‘j’.
   7.1 ‘i’ initialized as 0, ‘j’ initialized as ‘variable name of first string length result’.
   7.2 ‘i’ check upto ‘variable name of second string length result’-1.
   7.3 ‘j’ check upto ‘variable name of first string length result’ + ‘variable name of second string length result’
   7.4 Increment ‘i’ and ‘j’.
   7.5 Check for loop & must confirm it is in the format of “for(i=0,j=m;i<n-1,j<m+n;i++,j++)”.
   7.6 Initializations; Conditions ; In/Decrements.
8. Move output of second string value s2[i] to s1[j].
9. Print s1 by the help of puts(s1).

root@LAPTOP-KHULM439: ~/c

```
#include<stdio.h>
#include<string.h>
/* Dr.Arun Anoop M */
void main()
{
        char s1[100],s2[100];
        int i,j,m,n;
        printf("Enter the first string\n");
        scanf("%s",&s1);
        m=strlen(s1);
        printf("Enter the second string\n");
        scanf("%s",&s2);
        n=strlen(s2);
        for(i=0,j=m;i<n-1,j<m+n;i++,j++)
                s1[j]=s2[i];
        puts(s1);
}
```

```
root@LAPTOP-KHULM439:~/c# ./sstring
Enter the first string
Hello
Enter the second string
Hai
HelloHai
```

9. Read a string (ending with a $ symbol), store it in an array and count the number of vowels,consonants and spaces in it.

Count Line, Space, Characters:

The edit conversion code %[^\n] can be used as an alternative of gets.

scanf(" %[^`]s", input); //do not forget to put a space in scanf scanf(" %[^~]", input); //Enter a string in multiple lines terminated with ~

Concept:

1. /* Dr.Arun Anoop M */ This algorithm will help you to write program easily. Concept wise you must be strong.
2. Declare a string array of data type character 'char'.
3. Initialize i, line=0, word=0, char=0
4. Enter a string in multiple lines terminated with ~
   scanf(" %[^~]", input);
   After input giving, press '~'. Your program will consider it as end of your input string.
5. To count lines in text uptoend(string end is blackslash zero '\0').
6. Need to check 'not equal to end or \0' in for loop.
7. If new line '\n' identified , increment line and word.
8. Otherwise check 'space'. As we already know that space can represent either by '' or by '\t'.
9. If any space found, increment word and character by 1.
10. Otherwise increment character by 1.

root@LAPTOP-KHULM439: ~/c

```
#include<stdio.h>
#include<string.h>
/* Dr.Arun Anoop M */
void main()
{
        char s1[100];
        int i,line=0,word=0,chara=0;
        printf("Enter a string:~\n");
        scanf("%[^~]",s1);
        for(i=0;s1[i]!='\0';i++)
        {
                if(s1[i]=='\n')
                {
                        line++;
                        word++;
                }
                else
                {
                        if(s1[i]==' ' || s1[i]=='\t')
                        {
                                chara++;
                                word++;
                        }
                        else
                        {
                                chara++;
                        }
                }
        }
        printf("Character count is %d\n",chara);
        printf("Line count is %d\n",line);
        printf("Word count is %d\n",word);
}
```

```
root@LAPTOP-KHULM439:~/c# vi svcs.c
root@LAPTOP-KHULM439:~/c# ./svcs
Enter a string:~
hello hai
~
Character count is 9
Line count is 1
Word count is 2
```

Count Vowels, Consonants, Spaces:

Concept:

1. /* Dr.Arun Anoop M */ This algorithm will help you to write program easily. Concept wise you must be strong.
2. Declare a string array of data type character ‘char’.
3. Initialize i, v=0, c=0, s=0

4. Enter a string and read it using ‘gets’ function. Output string will consists of multiple words.
5. To count lines in text uptoend(string end is blackslash zero ‘\0’).
6. Need to check ‘not equal to end or \0’ in for loop.
7. If the entered string having “aeiou/AEIOU”, increment vowel count by 1. ‘OR’ gate used for “a/e/i/o/u/A/E/I/O/U”.
8. Else the entered string having ‘a-z/A-Z’, increment consonant by 1.
   8.1 a-z means in between a & z.
   8.2 String array s1[i] in between a & z AND A & Z.
   8.3 s1[i]>=’a’ && s1[i]<=’z’.
   8.4 s1[i]>=’A’ && s1[i]<=’Z’.
   8.5 Anyone among 8.3 and 8.4, Then increment c by 1.
9. If any space found, increment space by 1.
10. Print values.

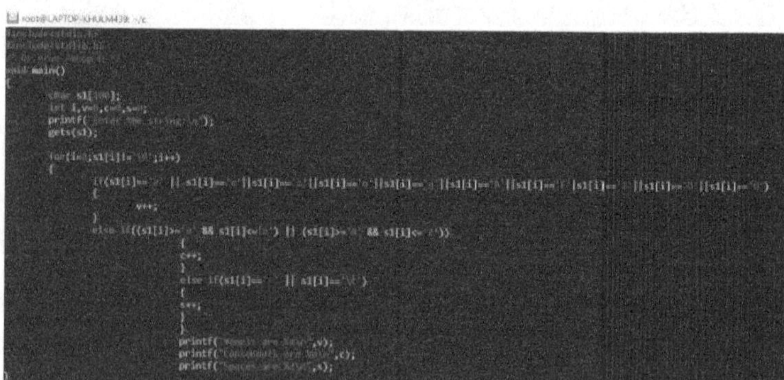

```
void main()
{
        char s1[100];
        int i,v=0,c=0,s=0;
        printf("[illegible]");
        gets(s1);

        for(i=0;s1[i]!='\0';i++)
        {
                if(s1[i]=='a' || s1[i]=='e'||s1[i]=='i'||s1[i]=='o'||s1[i]=='u'||s1[i]=='A'||s1[i]=='E'||s1[i]=='I'||s1[i]=='O'||s1[i]=='U')
                {
                        v++;
                }
                else if((s1[i]>='a' && s1[i]<='z') || (s1[i]>='A' && s1[i]<='Z'))
                        {
                        c++;
                        }
                        else if(s1[i]==' ' || s1[i]=='\t')
                        {
                        s++;
                        }
                }
                printf("[illegible]",v);
                printf("[illegible]",c);
                printf("[illegible]",s);
}
```

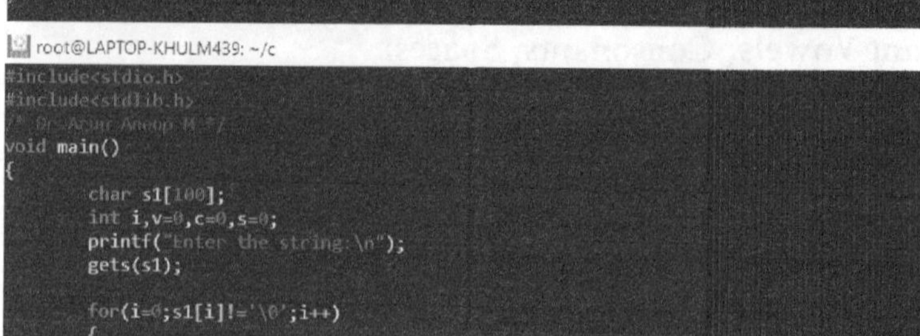

root@LAPTOP-KHULM439: ~/c

```
#include<stdio.h>
#include<stdlib.h>
/* Dr. Arun Anoop M */
void main()
{
        char s1[100];
        int i,v=0,c=0,s=0;
        printf("Enter the string:\n");
        gets(s1);

        for(i=0;s1[i]!='\0';i++)
        {
```

```
if(s1[i]=='a' || s1[i]=='e'||s1[i]=='i'||s1[i]=='o'||s1[i]=='u'||s1[i]=='A'||s1[i]=='E'|s1[i]=='I'||s1[i]=='O'||s1[i]=='U')
{
    v++;
}
```

```
else if((s1[i]>='a' && s1[i]<='z') || (s1[i]>='A' && s1[i]<='Z'))
            {
            c++;
            }
            else if(s1[i]==' ' || s1[i]=='\t')
            {
            s++;
            }
            }
            printf("Vowels are %d\n",v);
            printf("Consonants are %d\n",c);
            printf("Spaces are %d\n",s);
```

```
root@LAPTOP-KHULM439:~/c# ./vcs
Enter the string:
HOW ARE YOU
Vowels are 5
Consonants are 4
Spaces are 2
```

STRUCTURE: "A structure creates a data type that can be used to group items of possibly different types into a single type and keyword is 'struct'."

```
struct address
{
        char name[50];
        char street[100];
        char city[50];
        char state[20];
        int pin;
};
```

```
struct euclidian
{
int distance;     //data type member1
}dis,dis1;        // Variable1, Variable2,....variableN.
```

Later can access that by 'scanf("%d",&dis.distance)'.Accessing members of structures by using dot operator. Dot operator links structure variable to data member.

Structure variable . Structure Member;

10. Read two input each representing the distances between two points in the Euclidean space,store these in structure variables and add the two distance values.

Euclidian Distance formula is,

d=√((x_2-x_1)²+(y_2-y_1)²) to find the distance between any two points.

root@LAPTOP-KHULM439: ~/c

```
#include<stdio.h>
#include<math.h>
/* Dr.Arun Anoop.M */
void main()
{
        float x1,x2,y1,y2,d;
        printf("Enter Value for x_1:\n");
        scanf("%f",&x1);

        printf("Enter value for x_2:\n");
        scanf("%f",&x2);

        printf("Enter value for y_1:\n");
        scanf("%f",&y1);

        printf("Enter value for y_2:\n");
        scanf("%f",&y2);

        d=((x2-x1) * (x2-x1)) + ((y2-y1) * (y2-y1));
        printf("Euclidian Distance is %f\n",sqrt(d));
}
```

```
root@LAPTOP-KHULM439:~/c# gcc eucld.c -o eucld
/usr/bin/ld: /tmp/ccunkRc7.o: in function `main':
eucld.c:(.text+0x126): undefined reference to `sqrt'
collect2: error: ld returned 1 exit status
```

I struggled lots to solve this error. Finally I tried

```
root@LAPTOP-KHULM439:~/c# gcc eucld.c -o eucld -lm
root@LAPTOP-KHULM439:~/c# ./eucld
```

-lm is link against the math library.

```
root@LAPTOP-KHULM439:~/c# ./eucld
Enter Value for x_1:
3
Enter value for x_2:
-2
Enter value for y_1:
8
Enter value for y_2:
6
Euclidian Distance is 5.385165
```

```
        d=((x2-x1) * (x2-x1)) + ((y2-y1) * (y2-y1));
        printf("Euclidian Distance is %.4f\n",sqrt(d));
}
```

```
root@LAPTOP-KHULM439:~/c# gcc eucld.c -o eucld -lm
root@LAPTOP-KHULM439:~/c# ./eucld
Enter Value for x_1:
3
Enter value for x_2:
-2
Enter value for y_1:
8
Enter value for y_2:
6
Euclidian Distance is 5.3852
```

%.4f is "print as a floating point with a precision of four characters after the decimal point".

%4.3f is "print as a floating point at least 4 wide and a precision of 3".

root@LAPTOP-KHULM439: ~/c

```
#include<stdio.h>
/* Dr.Arun Anoop M*/
struct euclidiand
{
        int distance;
}dis,dis1;
void main()
{
        int sum=0;
        printf("Enter the distance between first two points:\n");
        scanf("%d",&dis.distance);
        printf("Enter the distance between second two points:\n");
        scanf("%d",&dis1.distance);
        sum=dis.distance+dis1.distance;
        printf("Total distance=%d\n",sum);
}
```

```
root@LAPTOP-KHULM439:~/c# ./euclidian
Enter the distance between first two points:
12
Enter the distance between second two points:
12
Total distance=24
```

11. Using structure, read and print data of n employees (Name, Employee Id and Salary)

1. Structure Declaration
2. Declare Structure variable
3. Read employees
4. Name read by the help of ‘gets’ function. Suppose if I type name ‘Arun Anoop’, I have to read Arun Anoop, must need gets function. Without that it will read up to Arun and stop.
5. Print Employee details. You already know the purpose of using dot operator.

root@LAPTOP-KHULM439: ~/c

```
#include<stdio.h>
#include<stdlib.h>
/* Dr.Arun Anoop M */
struct employee{
        char ename[40];
        int eid;
        float esal;
};
void main()
{
        struct employee emp;
        printf("Enter details of Employees:\n");

        printf("Enter Name:\n");
        gets(emp.ename);

        printf("ID:\n");
        scanf("%d",&emp.eid);

        printf("Salary:\n");
        scanf("%f",&emp.esal);

        printf("Entered detail is:\n");
        printf("Name is %s\n",emp.ename);
        printf("Id is %d\n",emp.eid);
        printf("Salary is %f\n",emp.esal);
}
```

```
Enter details of Employees:
Enter Name:
TOM & JERRY
ID:
1000
Salary:
200000
Entered detail is:
Name is TOM & JERRY
Id is 1000
Salary is 200000.000000
```

Another way is

root@LAPTOP-KHULM439: ~/c

```
#include<stdio.h>
#include<stdlib.h>
/* Dr Arun Anoop M */
struct employee{
        char ename[40];
        int eid;
        float esal;
}emp;
void main()
{
//      struct employee emp;
        printf("Enter details of Employees:\n");

        printf("Enter Name:\n");
        gets(emp.ename);


        printf("ID:\n");
        scanf("%d",&emp.eid);

        printf("Salary:\n");
        scanf("%f",&emp.esal);

        printf("Entered detail is:\n");
        printf("Name is %s\n",emp.ename);
        printf("Id is %d\n",emp.eid);
        printf("Salary is %f\n",emp.esal);
}
```

```
root@LAPTOP-KHULM439:~/c# ./emps1
Enter details of Employees:
Enter Name:
Jibin
ID:
1234
Salary:
100000
Entered detail is:
Name is Jibin
Id is 1234
Salary is 100000.000000
```

12. Declare a union containing 5 string variables (Name, House Name, City Name, State and Pincode) each with a length of C_SIZE (user defined constant). Then, read and display the address of aperson using a variable of the union.

Structure

1. Declare structure
2. Declare array of some size
3. Declare structure variable
4. Gets usage to read
5. Puts usage to print.

root@LAPTOP-KHULM439: ~/c

```c
#include<stdio.h>
/* Dr Arun Anoop M */


        struct person{
                char pname[50];
                char phouse_name[50], pcity[50],pstate[50],ppin[50];
        }p;
        void main()
        {
                printf("Enter the name of the person:\n");
                gets(p.pname);

                printf("Enter the House name:\n");
                gets(p.phouse_name);

                printf("Enter the City:\n");
                gets(p.pcity);

                printf("Enter the State:\n");
                gets(p.pstate);

                printf("Enter the pin code:\n");
                gets(p.ppin);

                printf("Entered details are:\n");
                        printf("Name you entered is:");
                        puts(p.pname);

                        printf("\nHouse Name is :");
                        puts(p.phouse_name);

                        printf("\nCity Name is:");
                        puts(p.pcity);

                        printf("\nState is:");
                        puts(p.pstate);

                        printf("\nPin code is :");
                        puts(p.ppin);
        }
```

```
root@LAPTOP-KHULM439:~/c# ./sper
Enter the name of the person:
Arun Anoop M
Enter the House name:
Krishnapriya
Enter the City:
Mattanur, Kannur
Enter the State:
Kerala
Enter the pin code:
670702
Entered details are:
Name you entered is:Arun Anoop M

House Name is :Krishnapriya

City Name is:Mattanur, Kannur

State is:Kerala

Pin code is :670702
```

Union

root@LAPTOP-KHULM439: ~/c

```
#include<stdio.h>
/* Dr.Arun Anoop M */
#define C_SIZE 100

        union person{
                char pname[C_SIZE];
                char phouse_name[C_SIZE], pcity[C_SIZE],pstate[C_SIZE],ppin[C_SIZE];
        };
        void main()
        {
                union person p;
```

root@LAPTOP-KHULM439: ~/c

```
#include<stdio.h>
/* Dr.Arun Anoop M */



        struct person{
                char pname[50];
                char phouse_name[50], pcity[50],pstate[50],ppin[50];
        }p;
```

root@LAPTOP-KHULM439: ~/c

```
#include<stdio.h>
/* Dr Arun Anoop M */
#define C_SIZE 100

        union person{
                char pname[C_SIZE];
                char phouse_name[C_SIZE], pcity[C_SIZE],pstate[C_SIZE],ppin[C_SIZE];
        };
        void main()
        {
                union person p;

                printf("Enter the name of the person:\n");
                gets(p.pname);

                printf("Enter the House name:\n");
                gets(p.phouse_name);

                printf("Enter The City:\n");
                gets(p.pcity);

                printf("Enter the State:\n");
                gets(p.pstate);

                printf("Enter the pin code:\n");
                gets(p.ppin);

                printf("Entered details are:\n");
                        printf("Name you entered is:");
                        puts(p.pname);

                        printf("\nHouse Name is :");
                        puts(p.phouse_name);

                        printf("\nCity Name is:");
                        puts(p.pcity);

                        printf("\nState is:");
                        puts(p.pstate);

                        printf("\nPin code is :");
                        puts(p.ppin);
        }
```

```
root@LAPTOP-KHULM439:~/c# ./sper1
Enter the name of the person:
Arun Anoop M
Enter the House name:
Krishnapriya
Enter the City:
Mattanur, Kannur
Enter the State:
Kerala
Enter the pin code:
670702
Entered details are:
Name you entered is:670702

House Name is :670702

City Name is:670702

State is:670702

Pin code is :670702
```

Program will print only Pin number 670702 because the union will hold only one value at a time.

13. Find the factorial of a given Natural Number n usingrecursive and non recursive functions

```
#include<stdio.h>
long int recursion(int n);
void main()
{
int n;
clrscr();
printf("Enter a positive integer: ");
scanf("%d",&n);
printf("Factorial of %d = %ld", n, recursion(n));
}
```

```
long int recursion(int n)
{
if (n>=1)
return n*recursion(n-1);
else
return 1;
}
```

Non recursive functions:

```
#include<stdio.h>
voidmain()
{
int i,fact=1,num;
printf("Enter a number: ");
scanf("%d",&num);
for(i=1;i<=num;i++){
fact=fact*i;
}
printf("Factorial of %d is: %d",num,fact);
}
```

root@LAPTOP-KHULM439: ~/c

```
#include<stdio.h>
/* Dr.Arun Anoop M */
long int factnonrec(int n)
{
        int i;
        long int fact=1;
        for(i=1;i<=n;i++)
                fact=fact*i;
        return fact;
}
```

```
long int factrec(int n)
{
	if(n==0)
		return 1;
	else
		return (n*factrec(n-1));
}
```

```
int main()
{
	int n;
	printf("Enter a number:\n");
	scanf("%d",&n);
	printf("Factiorial using non recursive function %ld\n",factnonrec(n));
	printf("factorial using recursive function %ld\n",factrec(n));
}
```

%ld means long integer displaying.

Combined one is added below

root@LAPTOP-KHULM439: ~/c

```
#include<stdio.h>
/* Dr.Arun Anoop M */
long int factnonrec(int n)
{
	int i;
	long int fact=1;
	for(i=1;i<=n;i++)
		fact=fact*i;
	return fact;
}
long int factrec(int n)
{
	if(n==0)
		return 1;
	else
		return (n*factrec(n-1));
}
int main()
{
	int n;
	printf("Enter a number:\n");
	scanf("%d",&n);
	printf("Factiorial using non recursive function %ld\n",factnonrec(n));
	printf("factorial using recursive function %ld\n",factrec(n));
}
```

```
root@LAPTOP-KHULM439:~/c# vi factr.c
root@LAPTOP-KHULM439:~/c# gcc factr.c -o factr
root@LAPTOP-KHULM439:~/c# ./factr
Enter a number:
4
Factiorial using non recursive function 24
factorial using recursive function 24
```

14. Read a string (word), store it in an array and obtain its reverse by using a user defined function.

```
#include<stdio.h>
#include<string.h>
void main()
{
char str[100],revstr[100];
int i,j=0;
//Take input string from user
printf("Enter a string:\n");
gets(str);
//To access each element from string in reverse order
for(i=strlen(str)-1;i>=0;i--)
{
revstr[j]=str[i];
j++;
}
printf("Reversed:\n");
puts(revstr);
}
```

15. Write a menu driven program for performing matrix addition, multiplication and finding thetranspose. Use functions to (i) read a matrix, (ii) find the sum of two matrices, (iii) find the productof two matrices, (i) find the transpose of a matrix and (v) display a matrix.

1. Readmatrix by &a[i][j].
2. Display matrix by a[i][j].
3. Add matrixc[i][j]=a[i][j]+b[i][j].
4. Transpose matrix c[j][i]=a[i][j].
5. Multiplication matrixc[i][j] += a[i][k] * b[k][j].
6. Use switch case in main function

6.1 m1==m2 && n1==n2(Size of Matrix A row and column m1,n1 &Size of Matrix B row and column m2,n2) for Matrix Addition.

6.2 n1==m2 for Matrix Multiplication.

$$\mathbf{A}+\mathbf{B}=\begin{bmatrix} a_{11} & a_{12} & \cdots & a_{1n} \\ a_{21} & a_{22} & \cdots & a_{2n} \\ \vdots & \vdots & \ddots & \vdots \\ a_{m1} & a_{m2} & \cdots & a_{mn} \end{bmatrix} + \begin{bmatrix} b_{11} & b_{12} & \cdots & b_{1n} \\ b_{21} & b_{22} & \cdots & b_{2n} \\ \vdots & \vdots & \ddots & \vdots \\ b_{m1} & b_{m2} & \cdots & b_{mn} \end{bmatrix}$$

$$= \begin{bmatrix} a_{11}+b_{11} & a_{12}+b_{12} & \cdots & a_{1n}+b_{1n} \\ a_{21}+b_{21} & a_{22}+b_{22} & \cdots & a_{2n}+b_{2n} \\ \vdots & \vdots & \ddots & \vdots \\ a_{m1}+b_{m1} & a_{m2}+b_{m2} & \cdots & a_{mn}+b_{mn} \end{bmatrix}$$

```
// Matrix Addition
#include<stdio.h>
#include<math.h>
void main()
{
int a[100][100],b[100][100],c[100][100],i,j,r,co;
printf("Enter dimension of matrix:");
scanf("%d%d",&r,&co);
printf("Enter Elements of first matrix:");
for(i=0;i<r;i++)
{
for(j=0;j<co;j++)
{
scanf("%d",&a[i][j]);
}
}
printf("Enter Elements of second matrix:");
for(i=0;i<r;i++)
{
for(j=0;j<co;j++)
{
```

```
scanf("%d",&b[i][j]);
}
}
for(i=0;i<r;i++)
{
for(j=0;j<co;j++)
{


//Addition of elements of two matrices
c[i][j]=a[i][j]+b[i][j];
}
}
printf("\nFirst Matrix:\n");
for(i=0;i<r;i++)
{
for(j=0;j<co;j++)
{
printf(" %d ",a[i][j]);
}
printf("\n");
}
printf("\nSecond Matrix:\n");
for(i=0;i<r;i++)
{
for(j=0;j<co;j++)
{
printf(" %d ",b[i][j]);
}
printf("\n");
}
printf("\nAddition of Matrices:\n");
for(i=0;i<r;i++)
```

```
{
for(j=0;j<co;j++)
{
printf(" %d ",c[i][j]);
}
printf("\n");
}
}
```

$$\mathbf{A} - \mathbf{B} = \begin{bmatrix} a_{11} & a_{12} & \cdots & a_{1n} \\ a_{21} & a_{22} & \cdots & a_{2n} \\ \vdots & \vdots & \ddots & \vdots \\ a_{m1} & a_{m2} & \cdots & a_{mn} \end{bmatrix} - \begin{bmatrix} b_{11} & b_{12} & \cdots & b_{1n} \\ b_{21} & b_{22} & \cdots & b_{2n} \\ \vdots & \vdots & \ddots & \vdots \\ b_{m1} & b_{m2} & \cdots & b_{mn} \end{bmatrix}$$

$$= \begin{bmatrix} a_{11} - b_{11} & a_{12} - b_{12} & \cdots & a_{1n} - b_{1n} \\ a_{21} - b_{21} & a_{22} - b_{22} & \cdots & a_{2n} - b_{2n} \\ \vdots & \vdots & \ddots & \vdots \\ a_{m1} - b_{m1} & a_{m2} - b_{m2} & \cdots & a_{mn} - b_{mn} \end{bmatrix}$$

//Matrix Substraction

SUBSTRACTION

```
#include<stdio.h>
#include<math.h>
void main()
{
int a[100][100],b[100][100],c[100][100],i,j,r,co;
printf("Enter dimension of matrix:");
scanf("%d%d",&r,&co);
printf("Enter Elements of first matrix:");
for(i=0;i<r;i++)
{
for(j=0;j<co;j++)
{
scanf("%d",&a[i][j]);
}
}
```

```
printf("Enter Elements of second matrix:");
for(i=0;i<r;i++)
{
for(j=0;j<co;j++)
{
scanf("%d",&b[i][j]);
}
}
for(i=0;i<r;i++)
{
for(j=0;j<co;j++)
{
c[i][j]=a[i][j]-b[i][j];
}
}
printf("\nFirst Matrix:\n");
for(i=0;i<r;i++)
{
for(j=0;j<co;j++)
{
printf(" %d ",a[i][j]);
}
printf("\n");
}
printf("\nSecond Matrix:\n");
for(i=0;i<r;i++)
{
for(j=0;j<co;j++)
{
printf(" %d ",b[i][j]);
}
printf("\n");
}
```

```
printf("\nSubtraction of Matrices:\n");
for(i=0;i<r;i++)
{
for(j=0;j<co;j++)
{
printf(" %d ",c[i][j]);
}
printf("\n");
}
}
```

$$\begin{bmatrix} a & b & c \\ d & e & f \\ g & h & i \end{bmatrix} \begin{bmatrix} j & k & l \\ m & n & o \\ p & q & r \end{bmatrix} = \begin{bmatrix} (aj+bm+cp) & (ak+bn+cq) & (al+bo+cr) \\ (dj+em+fp) & (dk+en+fq) & (dl+eo+fr) \\ (gj+hm+ip) & (gk+hn+iq) & (gl+ho+ir) \end{bmatrix}$$

MULTIPLICATION

```
#include<stdio.h>
#include<math.h>
void main()
{
int a[100][100],b[100][100],c[100][100],i,j,r1,r2,c1,c2,k;
clrscr();
printf("Enter dimension of first matrix:\nNumber of rows:");
scanf("%d",&r1);
printf("\nNumber of columns:");
scanf("%d",&c1);
printf("\nEnter dimension of second matrix:\nNumber of rows:");
scanf("%d",&r2);
printf("\nNumber of columns:");
scanf("%d",&c2);
if(r1!=c2)
{
printf("Multiplication is not possible!!!");
```

```
}
else
{
printf("Enter Elements of first matrix:");
for(i=0;i<r1;i++)
{
for(j=0;j<c1;j++)
{
scanf("%d",&a[i][j]);
}
}
printf("Enter Elements of second matrix:");
for(i=0;i<r2;i++)
{
for(j=0;j<c2;j++)
{
scanf("%d",&b[i][j]);
}
}
for(i=0;i<r1;i++)
{
for(j=0;j<c2;j++)
{
c[i][j]=0;
}}
for(i=0;i<r1;i++)
{
for(j=0;j<c2;j++)
{
for(k=0;k<c1;k++)
{
c[i][j]+=a[i][k]*b[k][j];
}
```

```
}
}
printf("\nFirst Matrix:\n");
for(i=0;i<r1;i++)
{
for(j=0;j<c1;j++)
{
printf(" %d ",a[i][j]);
}
printf("\n");
}
printf("\nSecond Matrix:\n");
for(i=0;i<r2;i++)
{
for(j=0;j<c2;j++)
{
printf(" %d ",b[i][j]);
}
printf("\n");
}
printf("\nMultiplication of Matrices:\n");
for(i=0;i<r1;i++)
{
for(j=0;j<c2;j++)
{
printf(" %d ",c[i][j]);
}
printf("\n");
}
}
getch();
}
```

$$A = \begin{bmatrix} a & b & c \\ d & e & f \end{bmatrix}_{2 \times 3} \qquad A^T = \begin{bmatrix} a & d \\ b & e \\ c & f \end{bmatrix}_{3 \times 2}$$

TRANSPOSE

```
#include <stdio.h>
void main() {
int a[20][20], trans[20][20], r, c, i, j;
printf("Enter rows and columns: ");
scanf("%d %d", &r, &c);
// Assigning elements to the matrix
printf("\nEnter matrix elements:\n");
for (i = 0; i< r; ++i)
{
for (j = 0; j < c; ++j)
{
printf("Enter element a[%d][%d]: ", i + 1, j + 1);
scanf("%d", &a[i][j]);
}
}
// Displaying the matrix a[][]
printf("\nEntered matrix: \n");
for (i = 0; i< r; ++i)
{
for (j = 0; j < c; ++j)
{
printf("%d  ", a[i][j]);
if (j == c - 1)
printf("\n");
}
}
// Finding the transpose of matrix a
```

```
for (i = 0; i< r; ++i)
{
for (j = 0; j < c; ++j)
{
trans[j][i] = a[i][j];
}
}
// Displaying the transpose of matrix a
printf("\nTranspose of the matrix:\n");
for (i = 0; i< c; ++i)
{
for (j = 0; j < r; ++j)
{
printf("%d  ", trans[i][j]);
if (j == r - 1)
printf("\n");
}
}
}
```

Based on algorithm, try to make all together program for Program number 15.

Matrix Transpose Steps

Initialize a_{1010},t_{1010},r,c,i,j; //{a_{1010} is a[10][10]}

I. Enter Matrix elements
   i->0 to r
   j->0 to c
   a11 a12 a13 a21 a22 a23
   a%d%d,i+1,j+1 //PRINTING TIME
   Read aij

II. Entered Matrix Printing
   i->0 to r
   j->0 to c

Print aij
if(j==c-1)
Print new Line

A13 {3==4-1; 3==3

Entered values will be in separate lines. We can arrange them in 3X2 order by using if(j==c-1) condition(Example rows=3,cols=2).

III. Compute Transpose
i->0 to r
j->0 to c
tji=aij

IV. Print Transpose
i->0 to c
j->0 to r
A21{2==3-1;2==2}
Print tij
To keep all values in 2X3 order, can give if(j==r-1) condition.

<u>Another Solution</u>

Step 1: Declare two 2 dimensional arrays.
Arrayname[row_size][column_size]
Row(r),Column(c),loop variable for row i, loop variable for column j.

Step 2: Read rows and columns

Step 3: Collect values for rows and columns

Step 4: Read first array(Need loop variables for rows and columns). {i is 0 to r, j is 0 to c}

Step 5: Use mathematical equation for transpose operation bij=aji within loops.

Step 6: Print bij (don't forget to declare for loops and its values must be within the specified rows and columns).

Step 7: If you want to show 2X2 matrix in correct form, use new line option "\n".

root@LAPTOP-KHULM439: ~

```
#include<stdio.h>
/* Dr.Arun Anoop M */
void main()
{
        int a[100][100],b[100][100],r,c,i,j;
        printf("Enter the rows and columns:\n");
        scanf("%d%d",&r,&c);
        printf("Enter number of elements:\n");
        for(i=0;i<r;i++)
        {
                for(j=0;j<c;j++)
                {
                        scanf("%d",&a[i][j]);
                }
        }
        for(i=0;i<c;i++)
        {
                for(j=0;j<r;j++)
                {
                        b[i][j]=a[j][i];
                }
        }
        for(i=0;i<c;i++)
        {
                for(j=0;j<r;j++)
                {
                        printf("%d",b[i][j]);
                }
                printf("\n");
        }
}
```

```
root@LAPTOP-KHULM439:~# vi trans.c
root@LAPTOP-KHULM439:~# gcc trans.c
root@LAPTOP-KHULM439:~# ./a.out
Enter the rows and columns:
2
2
Enter number of elements:
2
3
4
1
24
31
```

16. Do the following using pointers

i) add two numbers

ii) swap two numbers using a user defined function

ADDITION

1. Pointers pointing at a and b
2. Sum of a and b using pointers

```
#include<stdio.h>
void main()
{
int a,b,sum=0, *ptr_a, *ptr_b;
*ptr_a=&a;
*ptr_b=&b;
printf("Enter a and b:");
scanf("%d%d",&a,&b);
sum=*ptr_a+*ptr_b;
printf("\nSum = %d",sum);
}
```

SWAP

1. Declaration of variables and pointer variables
2. Insert value of x and y
3. Printing value before swapping
4. Assigning address of variables to pointers

5. Swapping pointer address with the help of temp variable
6. Printing values of x and y

```
#include<stdio.h>
 void main()
{
int x,y,*ptr_x,*ptr_y,temp;
printf("Enter the value of x and y\n");
scanf("%d%d", &x, &y);
printf("Before Swapping\nx = %d\ny = %d\n", x, y);
ptr_x = &x;
ptr_y = &y;
temp = *ptr_x;
*ptr_x = *ptr_y;
*ptr_y = temp;
printf("After Swapping\nx = %d\ny = %d\n", x, y);
}
```

17. Input and Print the elements of an array using pointers

1. Declaration of pointer and assigning array to it
2. Printing values of array using pointer

```
#include<stdio.h>
void main()
{
int arr[10],n,i;
int *ptr=arr;
printf("Enter the number of elements:\n");
scanf("%d",&n);
printf("\nEnter %d Elements:",n);
for (i=0;i<n;i++)
scanf("%d",&arr[i]);
printf("You entered: \n");
for (i=0;i<n;i++)
printf("%d\n",*(ptr+i));
```

```
}
```

18. Compute sum of the elements stored in an array using pointers and user defined function.

```
#include<stdio.h>
//Declaration of function ArraySum
int ArraySum(int arr[10],int n);
void main()
{
int arr[10],n,i;
int *ptr=arr;
printf("Enter the number of elements :\n");
scanf("%d",&n);
printf("\nEnter %d Elements:",n);
for (i=0;i<n;i++)
scanf("%d",&arr[i]);
//Calling function ArraySum and printing it's value
printf("\nSum = %d",ArraySum(arr,n));
}
//Definition of function ArraySum
int ArraySum(int arr[10],int n)
{
int i,sum=0;
for(i=0;i<n;i++)
sum+=arr[i];
return sum;
}
```

19. Create a file and perform the following

- **iii) Write data to the file**
- **iv) Read the data in a given file & display the file content on console**
- **v) append new data and display on console**

1. Variable to store user content
2. File pointer to hold reference to our file
3. fopen() return NULL if last operation was unsuccessful
4. File not created hence exit
5. Input contents from user to store in file

```
#include <stdio.h>
#include <stdlib.h>
void main()
{
   char data[1000];
   FILE * fPtr;
   fPtr = fopen("file1.txt", "w");
    if(fPtr == NULL)
   {
      printf("Unable to create file.\n");
      exit(EXIT_FAILURE);
   }
 printf("Enter contents to store in file : \n");
   fgets(data, 1000, stdin);
   fputs(data, fPtr); //Write data to file
   fclose(fPtr); // Close file to save file data
   printf("File created and saved successfully. :) \n");
}
```

APPEND

1. File pointer to hold reference of input file
2. Input file path to remove empty lines from user
3. Open all file in append mode.
4. fopen() return NULL if unable to open file in given mode.
5. Unable to open file hence exit
6. Input data to append from user
7. To clear extra white space characters in stdin

8. Append data to file
9. Reopen file in read mode to print file contents
10. Print file contents after appending string
11. Done with file, hence close file.
12. Reads a file character by character and prints on console.
13. @fPtr Pointer to FILE to read.

```
#include <stdio.h>
#include <stdlib.h>
void readFile(FILE * fPtr);
void main()
{
   FILE *fPtr;
   char filePath[100];
   char dataToAppend[1000];
   printf("Enter file path: ");
   scanf("%s", filePath);
   fPtr = fopen(filePath, "a");
   if (fPtr == NULL)
   {
      printf("\nUnable to open '%s' file.\n", filePath);
       printf("Please check whether file exists and you have write
privilege.\n");
      exit(EXIT_FAILURE);
   }
   printf("\nEnter data to append: ");
   fflush(stdin);
   fgets(dataToAppend, 1000, stdin);
   fputs(dataToAppend, fPtr);
   fPtr = freopen(filePath, "r", fPtr);
   printf("\nSuccessfully appended data to file. \n");
   printf("Changed file contents:\n\n");
   readFile(fPtr);
   fclose(fPtr);
```

```
}
void readFile(FILE * fPtr)
{
  char ch;
  do
  {
    ch = fgetc(fPtr);
    putchar(ch);
  } while (ch != EOF);
}
```

20. Open a text input file and count number of characters, words and lines in it; and store the resultsin an output file.

1. If file opened successfully, then write the string to file
2. Repeat until End Of File character is reached.
3. Increment character count if NOT new line or space
4. Increment word count if new line or space character
5. Increment line count if new line character

```
#include <stdio.h>
#include <stdlib.h>
void main()
{
 FILE *fp;
 char filename[100];
 char ch;
 int linecount, wordcount, charcount;
 linecount = 0;
 wordcount = 0;
 charcount = 0;
  printf("Enter a filename :");
  gets(filename);
   fp = fopen(filename,"r");
```

```
    if ( fp )
  {
  while ((ch=getc(fp)) != EOF) {
    if (ch != ' ' &&ch != '\n') {
                ++charcount;
                    }
     if (ch == ' ' || ch == '\n') {
            ++wordcount;
}
    if (ch == '\n') { ++linecount;
  }
  if (charcount> 0)
{     ++linecount;
    ++wordcount;
  }
   }
  else
    {
      printf("Failed to open the file\n");
      }
   printf("Lines : %d \n", linecount);
   printf("Words : %d \n", wordcount);
   printf("Characters : %d \n", charcount);
getchar();
}
```

SUMMARY

Images collected from various sources.

What is an Armstrong Number

$$1^3 + 5^3 + 3^3 = 153$$

The Fibonacci Sequence

1,1,2,3,5,8,13,21,34,55,89,144,233,377…

1+1=2	13+21=34
1+2=3	21+34=55
2+3=5	34+55=89
3+5=8	55+89=144
5+8=13	89+144=233
8+13=21	144+233=377

Fahrenheit and Celsius Conversion Formulas

Fahrenheit to Celsius:

$$C = (F - 32) \cdot \frac{5}{9}$$

Celsius to Fahrenheit:

$$F = C \cdot \frac{9}{5} + 32$$

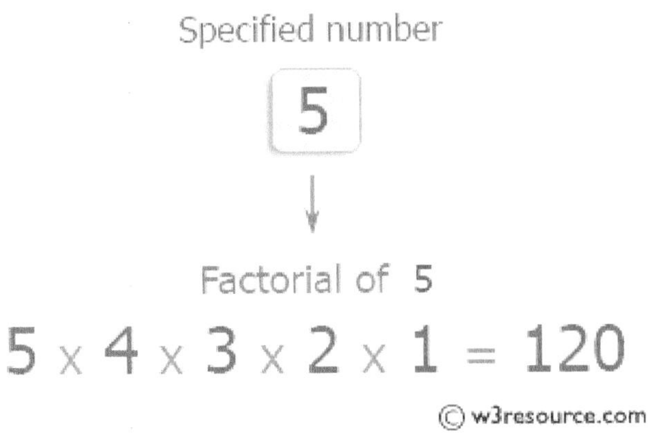

Prime Numbers

A number which only has two factors - itself and 1.

The first ten prime numbers are:
2 3 5 7 11 13 17 19 23 29

80	60	70	85	75
marks[0]	marks[1]	marks[2]	marks[3]	marks[4]

Initialization of Array

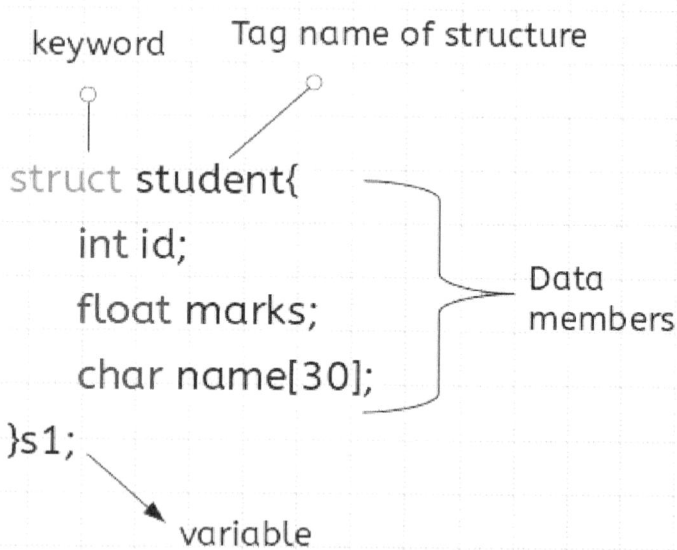

Function	Operation
fopen()	Creates a new file / opens an existing file
fclose()	Closes a file which has been opened for use
getc()	Reads a character from the file
putc()	Writes a character to the file
fprintf()	Write data values to a file
fscanf()	Reads a set of data values from a file
getw()	Reads an integer from the file
putw()	Writes an integer to a file
fseek()	Sets the position to the desired point in the file
ftell()	Gives the current position in the file
rewind()	Sets the position to the beginning of the file

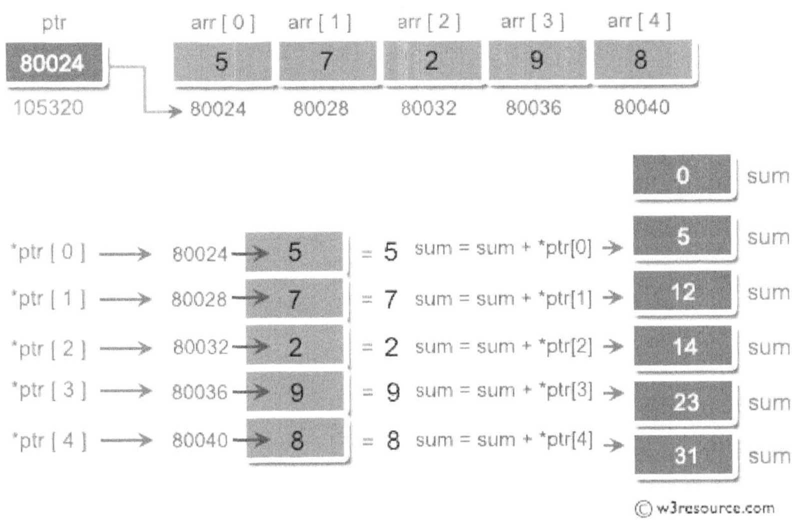

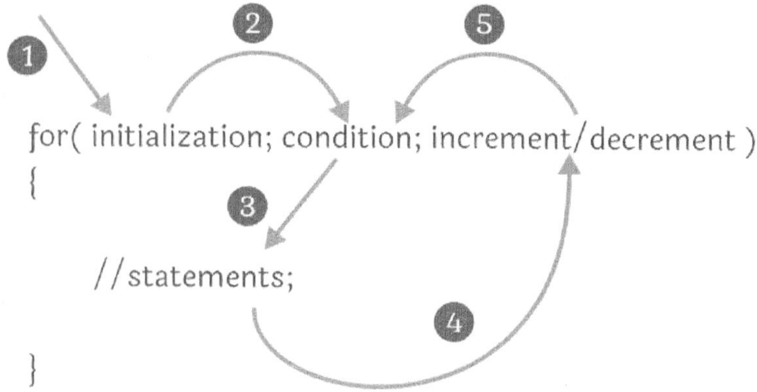

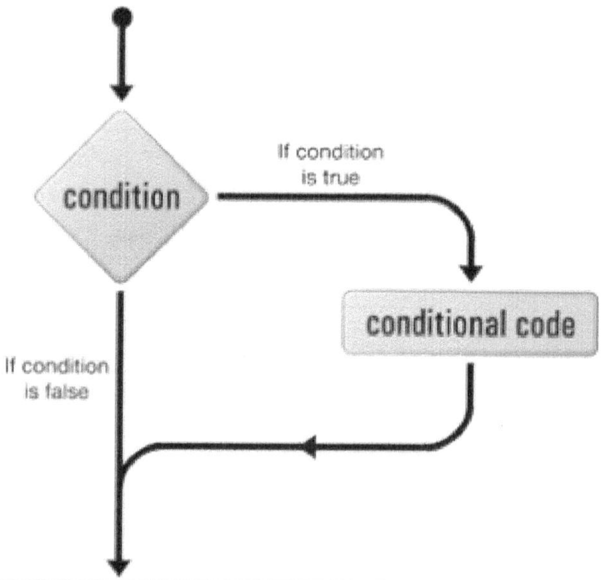

strlen	Finds length of a string
strlwr	Converts a string to lower case
strupr	Converts a string to uppercase
strcat	Appends one string at the end of another
strncat	Appends first n character of a string at the end of another
strcpy	Copies a string into another
strncpy	Copies first n character of one string into another
strcmp	Compares two strings
strncmp	Compares first n characters of two strings

```
if ( /*condition*/ ) {
    /*instructions*/
}
```

```
if ( /*condition*/ ) {
    /*instructions1*/
} else {
    /*instructions2*/
}
```

```
swich ( /*expression*/ ) {
    case 1:
        /*instructions1*/
        break;
    case 2;
        /*instructions2*/
        break;
    case 3;
        /*instructions4*/
        break;
}
```

```
while ( /*condition*/ ) {
    /*instructions*/
}
```

```
do {
    /*instructions*/
} while (/*condition*/);
```

```
for ( /*initialize_expression*/; /*test_expression*/; /*increment_expression*/) {
    /*instructions*/
}
```

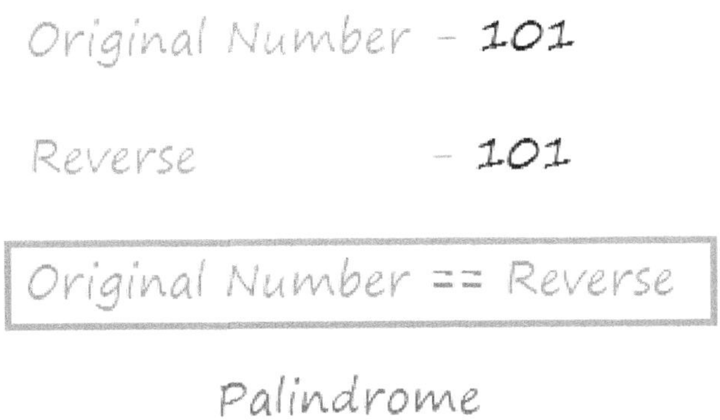

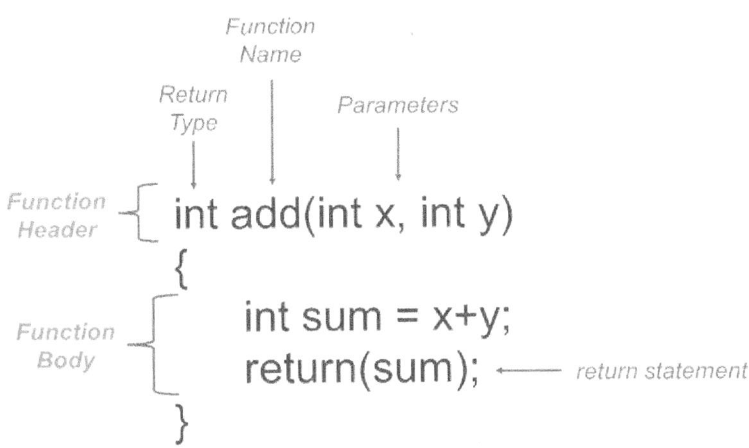

Leap Year or Not?

year % 100 == 0 && year % 400 == 0

year % 100 != 0 && year % 4 == 0

(c) Construct the nested if/else statement below into a switch case statement.

```
if (letter_grade == 'A')
        printf("Excellent!");
else if (letter_grade == 'B')
        printf("Very good!");
else if (letter_grade == 'C')
        printf("Good");
else if (letter_grade == 'D')
        printf("Adequate");
else
        printf("Fail");
```

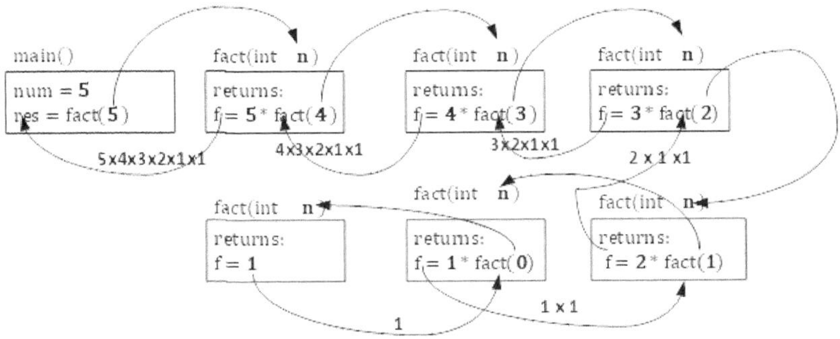
main()
num = 5
res = fact(5)
fact(int n)
returns:
f = 5 * fact(4)
fact(int n)
returns:
f = 4 * fact(3)
fact(int n)
returns:
f = 3 * fact(2)
5x4x3x2x1x1
4x3x2x1x1
3x2x1x1
2 x 1 x1
fact(int n)
returns:
f = 1
fact(int n)
returns:
f = 1 * fact(0)
fact(int n)
returns:
f = 2 * fact(1)
1
1 x 1

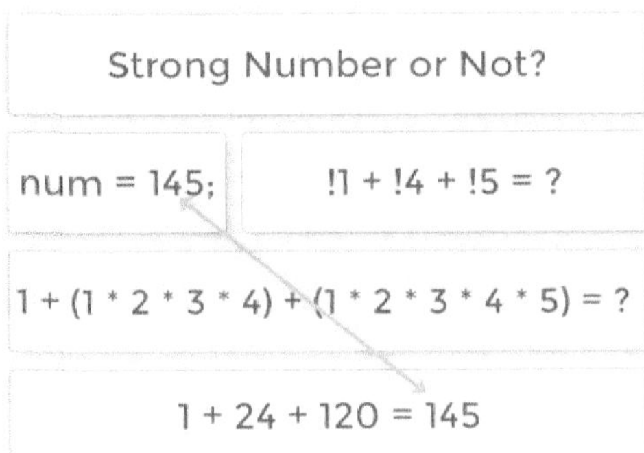
Strong Number or Not?
num = 145;
!1 + !4 + !5 = ?
1 + (1 * 2 * 3 * 4) + (1 * 2 * 3 * 4 * 5) = ?
1 + 24 + 120 = 145

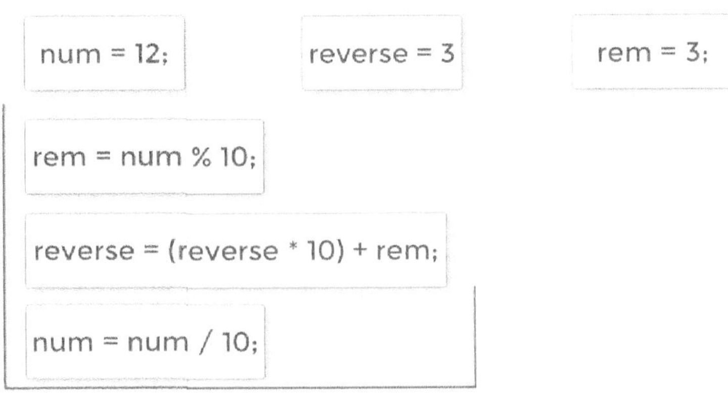
num = 12;
reverse = 3
rem = 3;
rem = num % 10;
reverse = (reverse * 10) + rem;
num = num / 10;

```
#include<stdio.h>
#include<conio.h>
void main() {
  int day;
  printf ("Enter the day of the week (1 to 7) ");
  scanf ("%d", &day);
  switch(day) {
    case 1 : printf ("Today is SUNDAY");break;
    case 2 : printf ("Today is MONDAY");break;
    case 3 : printf("Today is TUESDAY");break;
    case 4 : printf("Today is WEDNESDAY");break;
    case 5 : printf("Today is THURSDAY");break;
    case 6 : printf ("Today is FRIDAY");break;
    case 7 : printf("Today is SATURDAY");break;
    default : printf("Enter a valid choice(1 to 7 only)");
  }
  getch();
}
```

```
Enter the day of the week (1 to 7) 5
Today is THURSDAY
```

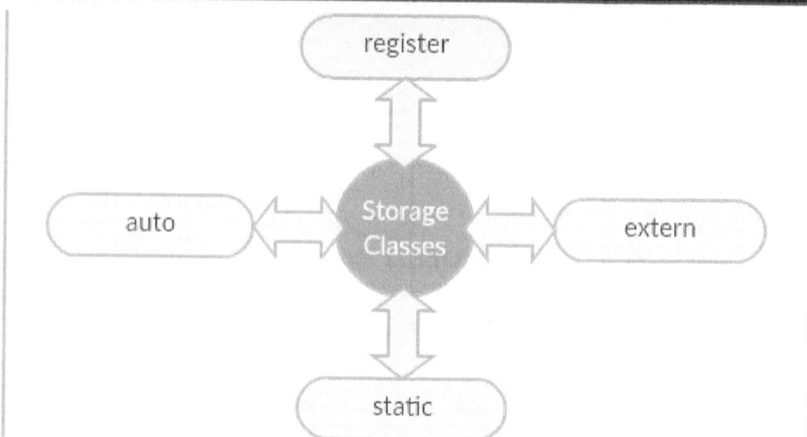

Item to be searched = 23

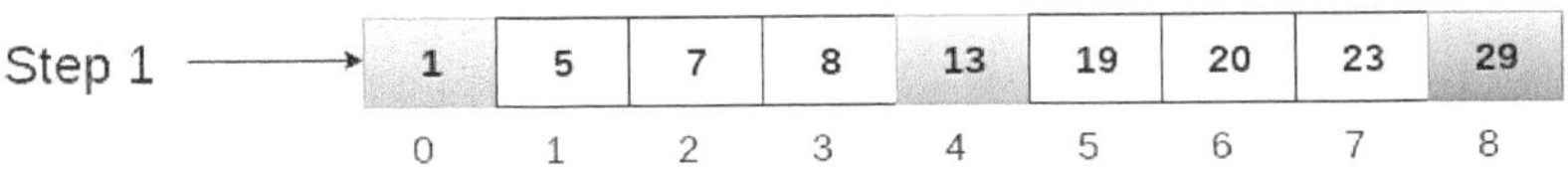

a [mid] = 13
13 < 23
beg = mid + 1 = 5
end = 8
mid = (beg + end)/2 = 13 / 2 = 6

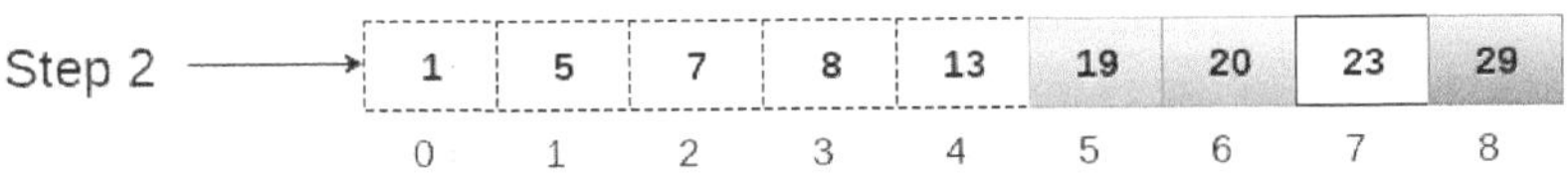

a [mid] = 20
20 < 23
beg = mid + 1 = 7
end = 8
mid = (beg + end)/2 = 15 / 2 = 7

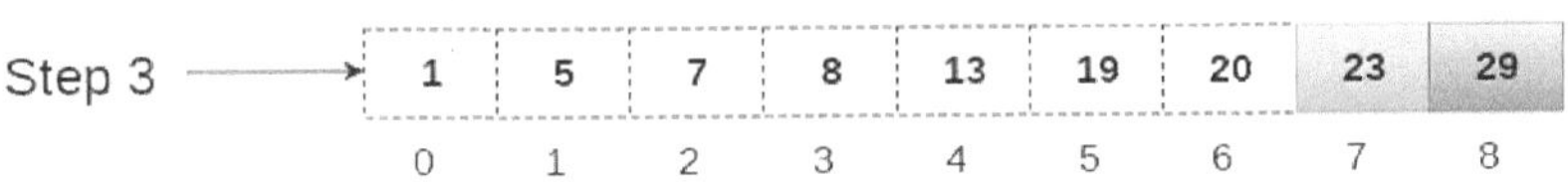

a [mid] = 23
23 = 23
loc = mid

Return location 7

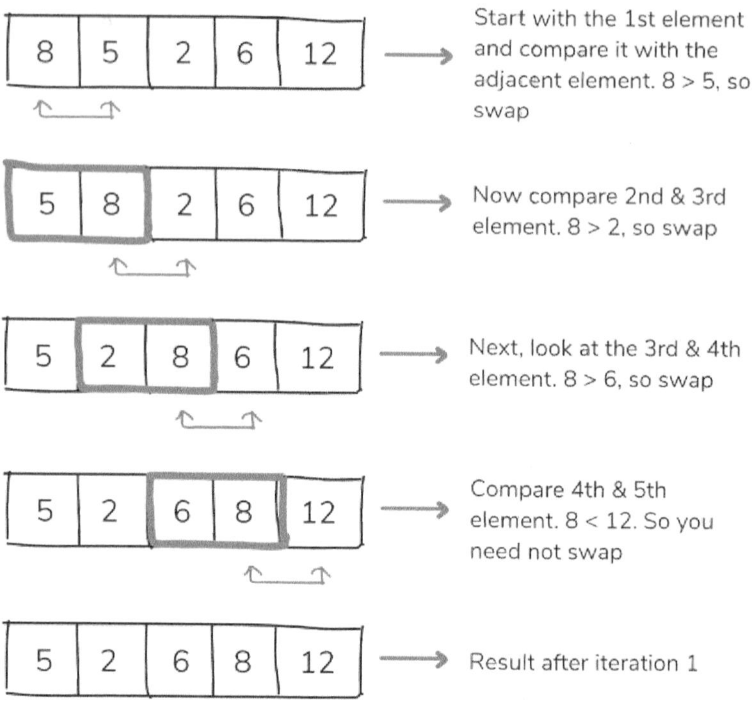
8 5 2 6 12
Start with the 1st element and compare it with the adjacent element. 8 > 5, so swap
5 8 2 6 12
Now compare 2nd & 3rd element. 8 > 2, so swap
5 2 8 6 12
Next, look at the 3rd & 4th element. 8 > 6, so swap
5 2 6 8 12
Compare 4th & 5th element. 8 < 12. So you need not swap
5 2 6 8 12
Result after iteration 1

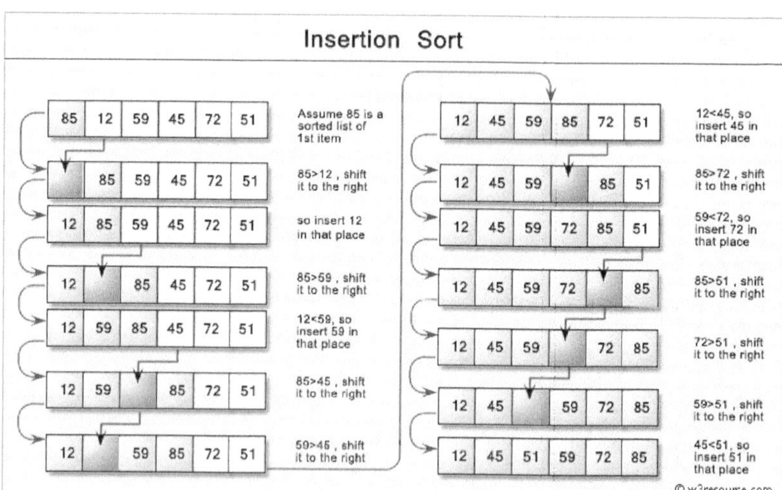
Insertion Sort
85 12 59 45 72 51
Assume 85 is a sorted list of 1st item
85 59 45 72 51
85>12 , shift it to the right
12 85 59 45 72 51
so insert 12 in that place
12 85 45 72 51
85>59 , shift it to the right
12 59 85 45 72 51
12<59, so insert 59 in that place
12 59 85 72 51
85>45 , shift it to the right
12 59 85 72 51
59>45 , shift it to the right
12 45 59 85 72 51
12<45, so insert 45 in that place
12 45 59 85 51
85>72 , shift it to the right
12 45 59 72 85 51
59<72, so insert 72 in that place
12 45 59 72 85
85>51 , shift it to the right
12 45 59 72 85
72>51 , shift it to the right
12 45 59 72 85
59>51 , shift it to the right
12 45 51 59 72 85
45<51, so insert 51 in that place
© w3resource.com

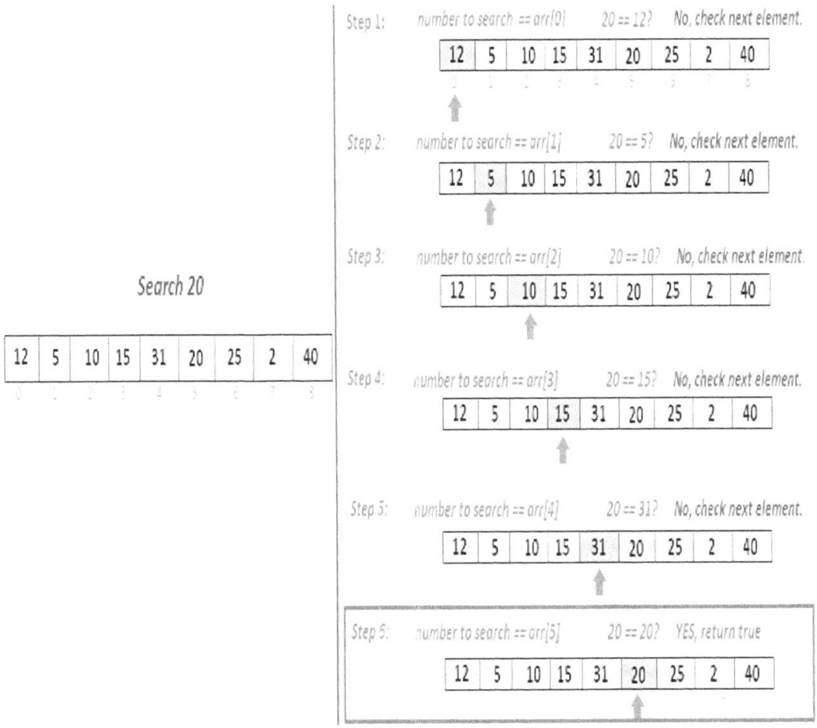
Search 20
12 5 10 15 31 20 25 2 40
Step 1: number to search == arr[0] 20 == 12? No, check next element.
Step 2: number to search == arr[1] 20 == 5? No, check next element.
Step 3: number to search == arr[2] 20 == 10? No, check next element.
Step 4: number to search == arr[3] 20 == 15? No, check next element.
Step 5: number to search == arr[4] 20 == 31? No, check next element.
Step 6: number to search == arr[5] 20 == 20? YES, return true

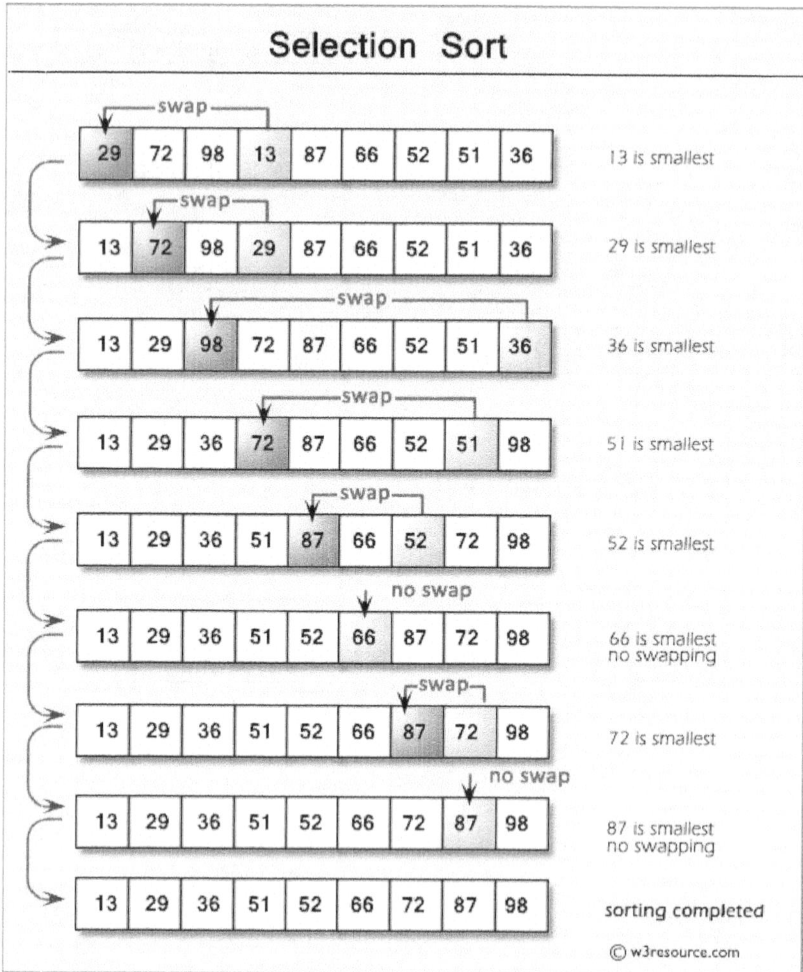
Selection Sort
swap
29 72 98 13 87 66 52 51 36
13 is smallest
swap
13 72 98 29 87 66 52 51 36
29 is smallest
swap
13 29 98 72 87 66 52 51 36
36 is smallest
swap
13 29 36 72 87 66 52 51 98
51 is smallest
swap
13 29 36 51 87 66 52 72 98
52 is smallest
no swap
13 29 36 51 52 66 87 72 98
66 is smallest
no swapping
swap
13 29 36 51 52 66 87 72 98
72 is smallest
no swap
13 29 36 51 52 66 72 87 98
87 is smallest
no swapping
13 29 36 51 52 66 72 87 98
sorting completed
© w3resource.com

REFERENCES

1) https://www.youtube.com/watch?v=LpuJZqV3juo&list=PLSzuwmVgelNxSi7pWzRTPOSiqdXHLI0GP&index=6
2) https://www.wikihow.com/Develop-Software#:~:text=%20Developing%20a%20Program%20%201%20Brainstorm%20ideas.,unexpected%20usage%20can%20cause%20all%20kinds...%20More%20
3) http://www.btechsmartclass.com/c_programming/C-Program-Development-Life-Cycle.html#:~:text=Program%20Development%20Life%20Cycle%201%20Problem%20Definition.%20In,5%20Testing%20%26%20Debugging.%20...%206%20Maintenance.%20
4) https://www.geeksforgeeks.org/introduction-to-algorithms/
5) https://online.visual-paradigm.com/diagrams/templates/flowchart/
6) https://www.hackingloops.com/linux-commands/
7) https://www.goeduhub.com/ (Program number 11-20 referred)
8) https://log4aman.wordpress.com/2014/03/13/623/
9) https://www.blendspace.com/lessons/VTIs3jHluYXvQg/learning-lesson-1
10) https://informationq.com/computer-hardware-basics-and-its-components/
11) https://www.indiamart.com/proddetail/computer-hardware-technician-course-14269655948.html
12) https://www.pinterest.com/pin/588986457493805385/
13) https://www.quotemaster.org/computer+hardware

14) https://www.epuzzle.info/en/puzzle/play/technology/83336-computer-hardware-and-software#7x4
15) https://www.integrity-online.ml/products.aspx?cname=computer+hardware+tools+list&cid=27
16) https://www.engworksheets.com/vocabulary-ready-new/preview/2/Computer-Parts/english-and-your-native-language-computer-parts-esl-printable-dictionary-worksheet-for-kids.html
17) https://www.smartdraw.com/flowchart/flowchart-symbols.htm
18) https://www.softwaretestinghelp.com/basics-of-computer-programming/
19) https://www.youtube.com/watch?v=pLnN3ooJcqw
20) https://www.cybermedian.com/comprehensive-guide-to-flowchart-with-50-examples/